ISBN 978-0-260-45899-5
PIBN 10949581

Historic, archived document

Do not assume content reflects current
scientific knowledge, policies, or practices.

UNITED STATES DEPARTMENT OF AGRICULTURE

Library

. 1, Revised   Washington 25, D. C., February 1952

SELECTED LIST OF AMERICAN AGRICULTURAL BOOKS

CONTENTS

This list of books in print is a revision of earlier lists with the same title. The inclusion of a title indicates no endorsement of the content of the book. Prices quoted have been taken from publishers' catalogs. Call numbers following the citations are those used in the United States Department of Agriculture Library.

BOSS, A., WILSON, H. K., and PETERSEN, W. E.,
American farming; Agriculture I-IV. St. Paul, Webb,
1941-50. 4 v. $16.00. V.1, rev. ed., 1950; v.2,1940;
v.3,1941; v.4,1944. 30.2 B65A
IOWA STATE COLLEGE OF AGRICULTURE AND ME-
CHANIC ARTS. Midwest farm handbook. Ed. 2.
Ames, Iowa State Col. Press, 1951. 280 p. $2.25.
30.3 Io9
WILCOX, E. V. Modern farmers' cyclopedia of agriculture; a compendium of farm science and practice on
field, garden, fruit and orchard crops, and the care,
feeding and diseases of farm animals. Ed. 2. New
York, Orange Judd, 1946. 511 p. $5.00. 30.1 W65M

AGRICULTURAL SCIENCE

Bacteriology

BREED, R. S., MURRAY, E. G. D., and HITCHENS, A. P.
Bergey's manual of determinative bacteriology. Ed.
6. Baltimore, Williams & Wilkins, 1948. 1529 p.
$15.00. 448.2 So12
BUCHANAN, E. D., and BUCHANAN, R. E. Bacteriology
Ed. 5. New York, Macmillan, 1951. 678 p. $6.00.
448.2 B852
BURDON, K. L. Textbook of microbiology. Ed. 3. New
York, Macmillan, 1947. 728 p. $3.50. 448.2 B892
CLIFTON, C. E. Introduction to the bacteria. New York,
McGraw-Hill, 1950. 528 p. $5.00. 448.2 C61
ELLIKER, P. R. Practical dairy bacteriology. New
York, McGraw-Hill, 1949. 391 p. $4.50. 448.2 EL53
HAMMER, B. W. Dairy bacteriology. Ed. 3. New York,
Wiley, 1948. 593 p. $6.00. 44 H182
HENRICI, A. T. Henrici's molds, yeasts, and actinomy-
cetes; a handbook for students of bacteriology. Ed. 2
by C. E. Skinner, C. W. Emmons, and H. M. Tsuchiya
New York, Wiley, 1947. 409 p. $5.00. 448.2 H39M
KELSER, R, A., and SCHOENING, H. W. Manual of vet-
erinary bacteriology. Ed. 5. Baltimore, Williams &
Wilkins, 1948. 767 p. $6.50. 448.2 K29
MERCHANT, I. A. Veterinary bacteriology and virology.
Ed. 4. Ames, Iowa State Col. Press, 1950. 885 p.
$8.50. 448.2 M53
RAHN, O. Microbes of merit. New York, Ronald, 1945.
277 p. $4.00. 448.2 R12Mi
SARLES, W. B., and others. Microbiology. New York,
Harper, 1951. 493 p. $4.50. 448.2 Sa72
W. C. Frazier, J. B. Wilson, and S. G. Knight, joint
authors.
SMITH, D. T., and FAGAN, L. T. Zinsser's textbook of
bacteriology. Ed. 9. New York, Appleton-Century-
Crofts, 1948. 992 p. $10.00. 448.2 Sm5
TANNER, F. W., and TANNER, F. W., JR. Bacteriology,
a textbook of microorganisms. Ed. 4. New York,
Wiley, 1948. 625 p. $5.00. 448.2 T15B

Biology; Zoology

BRELAND, O. P. Animal facts and fallacies. New York,
Harper, 1948. 268 p. $3.50. 411 B742
CLARK, A. H. Animals alive. New York, Van Nostrand,
1948. 472 p. $4.50. 411 C54A
GARRIGUS, W. P. Introductory animal science; ed by
R. W. Gregory. Philadelphia, Lippincott, 1951.
503 p. $5.50. 40 G192
GUYER, M. F. Animal biology. Ed. 4. New York, Har-
per, 1948. 780 p. $5.00. 411 G99
HALL, T. S. Source book in animal biology. New York,
McGraw-Hill, 1951. 716 p. $10.00. 442 H14
MAVOR, J. W. General biology. Ed. 3. New York, Mac-
millan, 1947. 986 p. $5.50. 442 M442
PARPART, A. K., ed. Chemistry and physiology of
growth. Princeton, Princeton U. Press, 1949. 293 p.
$4.50. 442 P242
PEARSE, A. S. Animal ecology. Ed. 2. New York,
McGraw-Hill, 1939. 642 p. $7.00. 411 P312
SHULL, A. F. Principles of animal biology. Ed. 6. New
York, McGraw-Hill, 1946. 425 p. $4.00. 442 Sh2
WOLCOTT, R. H. Animal biology. Ed. 3. New York,
McGraw-Hill, 1946. 719 p. $4.50. 411 W83

Botany

BAILEY, L. H. Manual of cultivated plants. Rev. ed.
completely restudied. New York, Macmillan, 1949.
1116 p. $17.50. 454 B15
CURTIS, O. F., and CLARK, D. G. An introduction to
plant physiology. New York, McGraw-Hill, 1950.
752 p. $6.50. 463.3 C94
DAUBENMIRE, R. F. Plants and environment. New
York, Wiley, 1947. 424 p. $4.50. 463.8 D26
EMERSON, F. W. Basic botany. Philadelphia, Blakiston,
1947. 372 p. $4.00. 463 Em3
FOSTER, A. S. Practical plant anatomy. Ed. 2. New
York, Van Nostrand, 1949. 228 p. $3.00. 463.41 F81
FRANCK, J., and LOOMIS, W. E., ed. Photosynthesis in
plants. Ames, Iowa State Col. Press, 1949. 500 p.
$7.00. 463.34 F84
FULLER, H. J. Plant world: a text in college botany.
Rev. ed. New York, Holt, 1951. 769 p. $4.75.
463 F952
HILL, A. F. Economic botany; a textbook of useful plants
and plant products. New York, McGraw-Hill, 1937.
592 p. $6.00. 452.8 H55
HILL, J. B., OVERHOLTS, L. O., and POPP, H. W.
Botany; a textbook for colleges. Ed. 2. New York,
McGraw-Hill, 1950. 710 p. $5.00. 463 H55
LAWRENCE, G. H. M. Keys to cultivated plants, families
and herbaceous genera. Ithaca, Bailey Hortorium,
Cornell U., 1946. 78 p. $3.00. 452 L43
MCDOUGALL, W. B. Plant ecology. Ed. 4, rev. Phila-
delphia, Lea & Febiger, 1949. 234 p. $4.00.
463.8 M142
MEDSGER, O. P. Edible wild plants. New York, Mac-
millan, 1931. 323 p. $3.75. 452.8 M46
MILLER, E. C. Plant physiology, with reference to the
green plant. Ed. 2. New York, McGraw-Hill, 1938.
1201 p. $10.00. 463.3 M61
MUENSCHER, W. C. L. Poisonous plants of the United
States. Rev. ed. New York, Macmillan, 1951. 277 p.
$4.00. 452.83 M92
ROBBINS, W. W., and WEIER, T. E. Botany; an introduction to plant science. New York, Wiley, 1950. 480 p.
$5.00. 463 R54B
STOVER, E. L. Introduction to the anatomy of seed
plants. Boston, Heath, 1951. 274 p. $4.00.
463.41 St7
SWINGLE, D. B. Textbook of systematic botany. Ed. 3.
New York, McGraw-Hill, 1946. 343 p. $3.50.
452.Sw5

Chemistry and Physics

ASSOCIATION OF OFFICIAL AGRICULTURAL CHEM-
ISTS. Official methods of analysis. Ed. 7. Washing-
ton, The author, 1950. 910 p. $10.00. 387 As720
BAILEY, A. E., ed. Cottonseed and cottonseed products.
New York, Interscience, 1948. 936 p. $10.00.
307 B15C
BAILEY, A. E. Industrial oil and fat products. Ed. 2,
rev. New York, Interscience, 1951. 967 p. $15.00.
307 B15
BROWNE, C. A. A source book of agricultural chemistry.
Waltham, Chronica Botanica, 1944. 290 p. (Chron-
ica Botanica V. 8, No. 1). $5.00. 450 C46
DUTCHER, R. A., JENSEN, C. O., and ALTHOUSE, P. M.
Introduction to agricultural biochemistry. New York
Wiley, 1951. 502 p. $6.00. 386 D95
FREAR, D. E. H., ed. Agricultural chemistry, a refer-
ence text. New York, Van Nostrand, 1950-51. 2 v.
v. 1, $9.00; v. 2, $9.50. 395 F87
GILBERT, F. A. Mineral nutrition of plants and animals.
Norman, U. Okla. Press, 1948. 131 p. $2.75.
395 G372
GORTNER, R. A. Outlines of biochemistry. Ed. 3. New
York, Wiley, 1949. 1078 p. $7.50. 386.2 G68
GREENBERG, D. M., ed. The amino acids and proteins.
Springfield, Ill., Thomas, 1951. 950 p.. $15.00.
387.1 G82
JACOBS, M. B. Chemical analysis of food and food prod-
ucts. Ed. 2. New York, Van Nostrand, 1951. 902 p.
$9.00. 389 J15

JACOBS, M. B., ed. Chemistry and technology of food and food products. Ed. 2. New York, Interscience, 1951. 3 v. V. 1, $12.00; v. 2, $15.00; v. 3, $15.00. 389 J15C

KAMEN, M. D. Radioactive tracers in biology: an introduction to tracer methodology. Ed. 2, rev. New York, Academic Press, 1951. 429 p. $7.50. 386.2 K122

MCNAIR, J. B. The analysis of fermentation acids. Los Angeles, Westernlore Press, 1947. 290 p. $7.50. 387.1 M23

SAHYUN, M. Outline of the amino acids and proteins. Ed. 2. New York, Reinhold, 1948. 286 p. $5.00. 386 Sa15

SCHWEITZER, G. K., and WHITNEY, I. B. Radioactive tracer techniques. New York, Van Nostrand, 1949. 241 p. $3.25. 386.2 Sch95

Mathematics and Statistical Methods

COCHRAN, W. G., and COX, G. M. Experimental designs. New York, Wiley, 1950. 454 p. $5.75. 251 C64

CROXTON, F. E., and COWDEN, D. J. Applied general statistics. New York, Prentice-Hall, 1939. 944 p. $6.35 trade ed.; $4.75 text ed. 251 C882A

EZEKIEL, M. Methods of correlation analysis. Ed. 2. New York, Wiley, 1941. 531 p. $6.00. 325 Ez3

FENSKE, T. H., DRAKE, R. M., and EDSON, A. W. Arithmetic in agriculture. St. Paul, Webb, 1951. 260 p. $1.00. 325 F36

IMMER, F. R. Applied statistics. Minneapolis, Burgess, 1950. 157 p. $3.25. 251 Im6

NADLER, M. Modern agricultural mathematics; a textbook for students of agriculture in high schools, vocational schools, and rural schools; and a handy reference book for farmers and other workers in various branches of agriculture, containing methods of calculation for all types of agricultural problems. New York, Orange Judd, 1940. 315 p. $2.00. 325 N12

PEARSON, F. A., and BENNETT, K. R. Statistical methods applied to agricultural economics. New York, Wiley, 1942. 443 p. $5.00. 251 P31

SNEDECOR, G. W. Statistical methods applied to experiments in agriculture and biology. Ed. 4. Ames, Iowa State Col. Press, 1946. 485 p. $5.00. 251 Sn2

Meteorology

BLAIR, T. A. Weather elements; a text in elementary meteorology. Ed. 3. New York, Prentice-Hall, 1948. 373 p. $5.65; $4.25 to schools. 340 B57

BYERS, H. R. General meteorology. New York, McGraw-Hill, 1944. 645 p. $7.00. 340 B99G

HAURWITZ, B., and AUSTIN, J. M. Climatology. New York, McGraw-Hill, 1944. 410 p. $6.00. 340 H29C

HEWSON, E. W., and LONGLEY, R. W. Meteorology, theoretical and applied. New York, Wiley, 1944. 468 p. $5.50. 340 H49

TREWARTHA, G. T. An introduction to weather and climate. Ed. 2. New York, McGraw-Hill, 1943. 373 p. $4.75. 340 T72

Breeding of Plants and Animals

ASDELL, S. A. Patterns of mammalian reproduction. Ithaca, Comstock, 1946. 437 p. $5.00. 444 As2

BABCOCK, E. B., and CLAUSEN, R. E. Genetics in relation to agriculture. Ed. 2. New York, McGraw-Hill, 1927. 673 p. $8.50. 442 B11

CASTLE, W. E. Mammalian genetics. Cambridge, Harvard U. Press, 1940. 169 p. $2.00. 443 C27M

CONFERENCE ON FERTILITY. The problem of fertility. Proceedings. Ed. by E. T. Engle. Princeton, Princeton U. Press, 1946. 254 p. $3.75. 444.9 C762

HAYES, H. K., and IMMER, F. R. Methods of plant breeding. New York, McGraw-Hill, 1942. 432 p. $5.50. 463.6 H32

LUSH, J. L. Animal breeding plans. Ed. 3. Ames, Iowa State Col. Press, 1945, 3d printing, 1949. 443 p. $4.00. 40 L972

PERRY, E. J., ed. The artificial insemination of farm animals. Ed. 2. rev. New Brunswick, Rutgers U. Press, 1947. 338 p. $4.00. 40 P942

RICE, V. A., and ANDREWS, F. N. Breeding and improvement of farm animals. Ed. 4. with a chapter on selection in meat animals by E. G. Warwick. New York, McGraw-Hill, 1951. 787 p. $7.00. 40 R36

SHULL, A. F. Heredity. Ed. 4. New York, McGraw-Hill, 1948. 311 p. $4.00. 442 Sh92H

SINNOTT, E. W., DUNN, L. C., and DOBZHANSKY, T. Principles of genetics. Ed. 4. New York, McGraw-Hill, 1950. 505 p. $5.00. 442 Si6

SNYDER, L. H. Principles of heredity. Ed. 3. Boston, Heath, 1946. 450 p. $4.00. 443 Sn9

WALTER, H. E. Genetics; an introduction to the study of heredity. Ed. 4. New York, Macmillan, 1938. 412 p. $4.60. 442 W17

WINTERS, L. M. Animal breeding. Ed. 4. New York, Wiley, 1948. 404 p. $4.50. 40 W73

GENERAL AGRICULTURE

BROMFIELD, L. Out of the earth. New York, Harper, 1950. 305 p. $4.00. 31.3 B780

BULLOCK, B. F. Practical farming for the South. Chapel Hill, U. N. C. Press, 2d printing, 1946. 526 p. $3.00. 31.3 B87

GRIMES, W. E., and HOLTON, E. L. Modern agriculture, based on "Essentials of the new agriculture," by Henry Jackson Waters. Rev. ed. Boston, Ginn, 1940. 646 p. $3.12. 30.2 G882

HAMMONDS, C., and WOODS, R. H. Today's agriculture. Ed. 3. Philadelphia, Lippincott, 1949. 522 p. $2.60. 30.2 H18

JACOBS, H. Practical guide for the beginning farmer. New York, Harper, 1951. 237 p. $3.00. 31.3 J15

KAINS, M. G. Five acres and independence; a practical guide to the selection and management of a small farm. Rev. and enl. ed. New York, Greenberg, 1944. 397 p. $2.50. 30 K123

LARSON, G. E., and TELLER, W. M. What is farming? New York, Van Nostrand, 1945. 410 p. $3.45. 31.3 L32

PEARSON, H. S. Successful part-time farming. New York, McGraw-Hill, 1947. 322 p. $3.25. 31.3 P312S Reprint available from Grosset & Dunlap for $1.49.

SCOTT, W., and PAUL, J. B. Permanent agriculture; a textbook of general agriculture. New York, Wiley, 1941. 614 p. $3.48. 30.2 Sco3

SMITH, J. R. Tree crops; a permanent agriculture. New York, Devin-Adair, 1950. 408 p. $6.00. 99 Sm6

TELLER, W. M. The farm primer; a manual for the beginner and part-time farmer. Philadelphia, McKay, 1942. 266 p. $3.00. 30.3 T23

U. S. DEPT. OF AGRICULTURE. Crops in peace and war, the yearbook of agriculture, 1950-1951. Washington, U. S. Govt. Print. Off., 1951. 942 p. $2.50. 1 Ag84Y

U. S. DEPT. OF AGRICULTURE. Science in farming, the yearbook of agriculture, 1943-1947. Washington, U. S. Govt. Print. Off., 1947. 944 p. $2.25. 1 Ag84Y

WILSON, C. M., ed. New crops for the new world. New York, Macmillan, 1945. 295 p. $3.75. 31 W69

FIELD CROPS

COPE, C. Front porch farmer. Atlanta, Smith, 1949. 171 p. $2.96. 31.3 C79

COX, J. F., and JACKSON, L. Field crops and land use. New York, Wiley, 1942. 473 p. illus. $4.50. 64 C83F

DUNGAN, G. H., and BOLIN, O. E. Judging crop quality. Danville, Ill., Interstate, 1950. 288 p. $3.50. 64 D91

FERGUS, E. N., HAMMONDS, C., and ROGERS, H. South-ern field crops management. Philadelphia, Lippincott 1944. 725 p. $3.40. 64 F38S

GRABER, L. F., and AHLGREN, H. L. Agronomy, principles and practices. Dubuque, Brown, 1948. 151 p. $2.25. 452.8 G76

GREGORY, R. W., ed. Field-crop enterprises. Rev. ed. Philadelphia, Lippincott, 1946. 552 p. $3.00. 64 D29

HUGHES, H. D., and HENSON, E. R. Crop production; principles and practices. New York, Macmillan, 1930. 813 p. $5.75. 64 H87

HUTCHESON, T. B., WOLFE, T. K., and KIPPS, M. S. The production of field crops; a textbook of agronomy Ed. 3. New York, McGraw-Hill, 1948. 430 p., illus. $5.00. 64 H97

KLAGES, K. H. W. Ecological crop geography. New York, Macmillan, 1942. 615 p. $6.00. 64 K66

MARTIN, J. H., and LEONARD, W. H. Principles of field crop production. New York, Macmillan, 1949. 1176 p., illus. $6.00. 64 M36

STATEN, H. W., and JONES, M. D. Farm crops: judging, identification and grading. Philadelphia, Blakiston, 1951. 251 p. $4.50. 64 St2

WILSON, H. K. Grain crops. New York, McGraw-Hill, 1948. 384 p. $4.00. 59 W69

KUMMER, A. P. Weed seedlings. Chicago, U., Chicago
Press, 1951. 435 p. $5.00. 454 K96
MUENSCHER, W. C. L. Weeds. New York, Macmillan,
1951[1935]. 579 p. $7.50. 79 M88
ROBBINS, W. W., CRAFTS, A. S., and RAYNOR, R. N.
Weed control; a textbook and manual. New York,
McGraw-Hill, 1942. 543 p. $5.50. 79 R53W
See also Plant Growth and Growth Substances.

HORTICULTURE

ADRIANCE, G. W., and BRISON, F. R. Propagation of
horticultural plants. New York, McGraw-Hill, 1939.
314 p. $4.50. 90.11 Ad8P
BAILEY, L. H., and BAILEY, E. Z. Hortus second; a con-
cise dictionary of gardening, general horticulture and
cultivated plants in North America. New York, Macmillan, 1941. 778 p. $6.00. 90.01 B15H
BAILEY, L. H., ed. The standard cyclopedia of horticul-
ture. New ed. New York, Macmillan, 1925. 3 v.
$37.00. 90.01 B15S
EDMOND, J. B., MUSSER, A. M., and ANDREWS, F. S.
Fundamentals of horticulture; a textbook designed for
courses in general horticulture. Philadelphia,
Blakiston, 1951. 502 p. $5.50. 90.4 Ed5
GARDNER, V. R. Basic horticulture. Rev. ed. New
York, Macmillan, 1951. 465 p. $4.75. 90.4 G17
GARRIS, E. W., and WOLFE, H. S. Southern horticulture
management. Philadelphia, Lippincott, 1949. 564 p.
$3.40. 90.2 G19S
GREGORY, R. W., ed. Horticulture enterprises, by
W. B. Balch, A. S. Colby, and T. J. Talbert. Rev.
Philadelphia, Lippincott, 1949. 480 p. $3.00.
90.4 G86
KAINS, M. G., and MCQUESTEN, L. M. Propagation of
plants; a complete guide for professional and am-
ateur growers of plants by seeds, layers, grafting and
budding, with chapters on nursery and greenhouse
management. Rev. and enl. ed. New York, Orange
Judd, 1942. 640 p. $4.50. 90.11 K12
TALBERT, T. J. General horticulture; principles and
practices of orchard, small fruit, and garden culture.
Philadelphia, Lea & Febiger, 1946. 452 p. $4.00.
93 T14G
TAYLOR, N., ed. Taylor's encyclopedia of gardening,
horticulture and landscape design. Ed. 2, rev. & enl.,
of the Garden Dictionary. New York, Amer. Garden
Guild and Houghton, Mifflin, 1948. 1225 p. $5.00.
90.01 T21

Greenhouses and Greenhouse Cultivation

CHABOT, E. D. Greenhouse gardening for everyone.
New York, Barrows, 1946. 266 p. $4.00. 90.13 C34
WRIGHT, W. J. Greenhouses; their construction and
equipment. Rev. ed. New York, Orange Judd, 1946.
269 p. $2.50. 90.14 W93

Home Gardening

BAILEY, L. H. Gardener's handbook... Brief indications
for the growing of common flowers, vegetables and
fruit in the garden and about the home. Imperial ed.
New York, Macmillan, 1934. 292 p. $2.49.
90.02 B15G
BETTER HOMES AND GARDENS. Garden book; a year-
round guide to practical home gardening. Des Moines
Meredith, 1951. 480 p. $3.95. 90 B463G
CLARKSON, R. E. Herbs, their culture and uses. New
York, Macmillan, 1942. 226 p. $3.75. 97.21 C56H
DE GRAAFF, J. The new book of lilies. New York,
Barrows, 1951. 176 p. $3.50. 96.46 D36
FREE, M. All about house plants; their selection, cul-
ture and propagation, and how best to use them for
decorative effect. Garden City, Doubleday and
American Garden Guild, 1946. 329 p. $3.50.
96.06 F87
FREE, M. Gardening; a complete guide to garden making
including flowers and lawns, trees and shrubs, fruits
and vegetables, plants in the home and greenhouse.
Rev. ed. New York, Harcourt, Brace and Amer. Gar-
den Guild, 1947. 550 p. $4.75. 90 F87
GUNNISON, O. M. Learning to garden. New York, Funk,
1948. 388 p. 97 G95
HASTINGS, L., and HASTINGS, D. The southern garden
book. Garden City, Doubleday, 1948. 276 p. $4.95.
90.1 H27
HOTTES, A. C. Book of annuals. Ed. 5, rev. New York,
De La Mare, 1945. 172 p. $2.00. 97.41 H79
HOTTES, A. C. Book of perennials. New York,
De la Mare, 1950. 272 p. $2.75. 97.42 H79P

HOTTES, A. C. 1001 garden questions answered. Ed. 4. New York, De la Mare, 1951. 381 p. $3.50. 90.02 H79

JENKINS, D. H. The weekend gardener. New York, Rinehart, 1950. 280 p. $2.75. 90.3 J41

MCFARLAND, J. H., and PYLE, R. How to grow roses. Ed. 22. New York, Macmillan, 1948. 192 p. $2.49. 96.1 C742

MINER, B. B. How to grow flowers, vegetables and fruit trees in your garden. New York, Grosset & Dunlap, 1950[1948]. 92 p. $1.00. 90.1 M66

MORSE, H. K. Gardening in the shade. New York, Scribner, 1939. 205 p. $5.00. 97.2 M83

PELLETT, F. C. Success with wild flowers. New York, De la Mare, 1948. $2.50. 97.12 P362

POST, K. Plants and flowers in the home. New York, Orange Judd, 1944. 198 p. $2.50. 96.06 P84

SCRUGGS, MRS. G. R., and SCRUGGS, M. A. Gardening in the South and West. Garden City, Doubleday, 1947. 297 p. $3.00. 97 Scr6

SIMON, M. J., and others. The complete garden hand-book. New York, Van Nostrand, 1950. 451 p. $5.00. 90 Si52
    D. W. Pierce, B. P. Hendrix, and J. Elliott, joint authors.

TABOR, G. Making a garden of perennials. New York, McBride, 1951. 96 p. $1.50. 97.42 T11

WISTER, J. C. Bulbs for home gardens. New York, Oxford U. Press, 1948. 270 p. $5.00. 96.4 M88

Hydroponics

GERICKE, W. F. The complete guide to soilless gardening. New York, Prentice-Hall, 1940. 285 p. $3.75. 90.15 G31

TURNER, W. I., and HENRY, V. M. Growing plants in nutrient solutions. New York, Wiley, 1939. 154 p. $3.50. 90.15 T85

Vegetables

BROWN, H. D., and HUTCHISON, C. S. Vegetable science. Philadelphia, Lippincott, 1949. 452 p. $5.50. 91.13 B81

COSPER, L. C., and LOGAN H. B. How to grow vegetables. New York, Duell, Sloan & Pearce, 1951. 263 p. $3.50. 91.15 C822

DEMPSEY, P. W. Grow your own vegetables. Rev. ed. Boston, Houghton, Mifflin, 1944. 220 p. $2.50. 91.15 D39

KNOTT, J. E. Vegetable growing. Ed. 4. Philadelphia, Lea & Febiger, 1949. 314 p. $4.00. 91 K75

THOMPSON, H. C. Vegetable crops. Ed. 4. New York, McGraw-Hill, 1949. 611 p. $6.00. 91 T372

WATTS, R. L., and WATTS, G. S. The vegetable growing business. Rev. ed. New York, Orange Judd, 1949. 542 p. $4.00. 91 W34Vg

WORK, P. Vegetable production and marketing. New York, Wiley, 1945. 559 p. $3.60. 91 W89

Specific Vegetables

COMIN, D. Onion production. New York, Orange Judd, 1946. 186 p. $2.00. 91.44 C73

HARDENBURG, E. V. Potato production. Ithaca, Comstock, 1949. 270 p. $3.00. 75 H21P

THOMPSON, H. C. Asparagus production. New York, Orange Judd, 1942. 124 p. $1.50. 91.41 T37

WORK, P. The tomato. New York, Orange Judd, 1942. 185 p. $1.75. 91.58 W89T

Fruits

AUCHTER, E. C., and KNAPP, H. B. Orchard and small fruit culture. Ed. 3. New York, Wiley, 1937. 627 p. $5.50. 93.21 Au2

CHANDLER, W. H. Deciduous orchards. Ed. 2. Philadelphia, Lea & Febiger, 1951. 436 p. $6.50. 93 C362

CHANDLER, W. H. Evergreen orchards. Philadelphia, Lea & Febiger, 1950. 452 p. $6.00. 93.4 C36

CHILDERS, N. F. Fruit science, orchard, and small fruit management. Philadelphia, Lippincott, 1949. 630 p. $5.50. 93.21 C432

HEDRICK, U. P. Fruits for the home garden. New York, Oxford U. Press, 1944. 171 p. $3.50. 93.21 H35Fr

KNAPP, H. B., and AUCHTER, E. C. Growing tree and small fruits. Ed. 2. New York, Wiley, 1941. 615 p. $3.60. 93.21 K72

SOUTHWICK, L. Dwarf fruit trees. Ed. by Ed. Robinson. New York, Macmillan, 1948. 126 p. $1.49. 93.5 So8

Specific Fruits

GARDNER, V. R. The cherry and its culture. Rev. ed. New York, Orange Judd, 1946. 146 p. $1.75. 93.32 G17

HEDRICK, U. P. Grapes and wines from home vineyards. New York, Oxford U. Press, 1945. 326 p. $4.00. 95.2 H35

HUME, H. H. The cultivation of citrus fruits. New York, Macmillan, 1926. 561 p. $6.00. 93.33 H88C

LLOYD, J. W. Muskmelon production. New York, Orange Judd, 1928. 126 p. $1.75. 91.51 L77

SMOCK, R. M., and NEUBERT, A. M. Apples and apple products. New York, Interscience, 1950. 486 p. $7.80. 93.31 Sm7

TUKEY, H. B. The pear and its culture. New York, Orange Judd, 1928. 125 p. $1.75. 93.36 T81

VANDER BOOM, M. M. Our American orange. New York, Didier, 1951. 63 p. $2.75. 93.331 V28

WAGNER, P. M. A wine-grower's guide. New York, Knopf, 1945. 230 p. $3.00. 95.2 W12

WEBBER, H. J., and BATCHELOR, L. D., ed. Citrus industry. Berkeley, U. Calif. Press, 1943-48. 2 v. $10.00 each. 93.33 W38

Nuts

BUSH, C. D. Nut grower's handbook. New York, Orange Judd, 1941. 189 p. $2.50. 94.6 B96

Floriculture - Commercial

DURUZ, W. P. Principles of nursery management. New York, De la Mare, 1950. 125 p. $3.50. 90.21 D93

LAURIE, A., and KIPLINGER, D. C. Commercial flower forcing. Ed. 5. Philadelphia, Blakiston, 1948. 550 p. $5.00. 90.13 L37

LAURIE, A., and RIES, V. H. Floriculture, fundamentals and practices. Ed. 2. New York, McGraw-Hill, 1950. 525 p. $5.50. 97.4 L37

POST, K. Florist crop production and marketing; the application of scientific facts to the production and marketing of florist cut flowers, potted plants, and bulbs grown in the greenhouse or in the field. New York, Orange Judd, 1949. 891 p. $10.00. 96.04 P84

Shrubs, Trees, and Vines

BAILEY, L. H. Cultivated conifers in North America. New York, Macmillan, 1933. 404 p. $12.00. 97.32 B15C

FELT, E. P. Our shade trees. Ed. 2. New York, Orange Judd, 1942. 316 p. $3.50. 97.7 F34

HOTTES, A. C. The book of shrubs. Ed. 5. New York, De la Mare, 1950. 438 p. $4.00. 97.31 H79

HOTTES, A. C. The book of trees. Ed. 2. New York, De la Mare, 1942. 440 p. $4.00. 97.7 H79

HOTTES, A. C. Climbers and ground covers; including the vast array of hardy and subtropical vines which climb or creep. New York, De la Mare, 1947. 302 p. $3.00. 97.43 H79

PIRONE, P. P. Maintenance of shade and ornamental trees. Ed. 2, rev. and enl. New York, Oxford U. Press, 1948. 436 p. $7.00. 97.7 P66

REHDER, A. Manual of cultivated trees and shrubs hardy in North America, exclusive of the subtropical and warmer temperate regions. Ed. 2, rev. New York, Macmillan, 1940. 996 p. $12.50. 452 R26

TABOR, G. Making the grounds attractive with shrubs. New York, McBride, 1950. 94 p. $1.00. 97.31 T11M

WYMAN, D. Shrubs and vines for American gardens. New York, Macmillan, 1949. 442 p. $7.50. 97.3 W98

WYMAN, D. Trees for American gardens. New York, Macmillan, 1951. 376 p. $7.50. 97.3 W98T

Landscape Gardening

BOTTOMLEY, M. E. New designs of small properties. Rev. ed. New York, Macmillan, 1948. 174 p. $4.00. 98 B65

ELLIOTT, J. 65 practical garden plans. New York, Van Nostrand, 1950. 38 p. $1.00. 98 EL53

JOHNSON, L. R. How to landscape your grounds. Ed. 2. New York, De la Mare, 1950. 257 p. $3.50. 98 J62

ORTLOFF, H. S., and RAYMORE, H. B. Color and design for every garden. New York, Barrows, 1951. 301 p. $3.50. 97.2 Or8C

ORTLOFF, H. S., and RAYMORE, H. B. Garden planning and building. Rev. ed. Garden City, Doubleday, 1945. 282 p. $3.50. 98 Or8

SPRAGUE, H. B. Better lawns. Garden City, Doubleday, 1945[1940]. 205 p. $2.00. 97.6 Sp7
VAN DE BOE, L. Planning and planting your own place. New York, Macmillan, 1947. 290 p. $2.95. 98 V28

Pruning

BAILEY, L. H. The pruning manual, being the 18th ed., rev. and reset, of the Pruning book. New York, Macmillan, 1916. 407 p. $4.00. 90.12 B15
FELT, E. P. Pruning trees and shrubs. New York, Orange Judd, 1941. 237 p. $2.50. 99.49 F34

FORESTRY

ALLEN, S. W. An introduction to American forestry. Ed. 2. New York, McGraw-Hill, 1950. 413 p. $4.50. 99 AL5
BAKER, F. S. Principles of silviculture. New York, McGraw-Hill, 1950. 414 p. $5.00. 99.45 B17P
BALDWIN, H. I. Forest tree seed of the north temperate regions, with special reference to North America. Waltham, Chronica Botanica, 1942. 240 p. (Plant Science Books, n. s. v. 8). $5.00. 61 B192
BRAUN, E. L. Deciduous forests of eastern North America. Philadelphia, Blakiston, 1950. 596 p. $10.00. 99.11 B73
BROWN, H. P., PANSHIN, A. J., and FORSAITH, C. C. Textbook of wood technology. V. 1, Structure, identification, defects, and uses of the commercial woods of the United States. New York, McGraw-Hill, 1949. 634 p. $6.50. 99.79 B81T
BROWN, N. C. Forest products; the harvesting, processing, and marketing of materials other than lumber, including the principal derivatives, extractives, and incidental products in the United States and Canada. New York, Wiley, 1950. 399 p. $5.00. 99.75 B81F
BROWN, N. C. Logging. New York, Wiley, 1949. 418 p. $5.50. 99.76 B81
BROWN, N. C. Lumber. New York, Wiley, 1947. 344 p. $4.75. 99.76 B81Lu
BRUCE, D., and SCHUMACHER, F. X. Forest mensuration. Ed. 3. New York, McGraw-Hill, 1950. 483 p. $5.00. 99.4 B83
BUTTRICK, P. L. Forest economics and finance. New York, Wiley, 1943. 484 p. $5.50. 99.7 B98
CHAPMAN, H. H. Forest management. New ed. Bristol, Conn., Hildreth Press, 1950. 582 p. $6.00. 99.55 C36
CHAPMAN, H. H., and MEYER, W. H. Forest valuation. New York, McGraw-Hill, 1947. 521 p. $6.00. 99.57 C36F
COLLINGWOOD, G. H. Knowing your trees. Rev. ed. Washington, Amer. Forestry Assoc. 1951[1947] 312 p. $5.00. 99.3 C69
GLESINGER, E. The coming age of wood. New York, Simon & Schuster, 1949. 279 p. $3.50. 99.75 G48
GREELEY, W. B. Forests and men. New York, Doubleday, 1951. 255 p. $3.00. 99.04 G81
GUISE, C. H. The management of farm woodlands. Ed. 2. New York, McGraw-Hill, 1950. 356 p. $4.00. 99.55 G94
GULICK, L. H. American forest policy; a study of government administration and economic control. New York, Duell, Sloan and Pearce, 1951. 252 p. $3.50. 99.61 G94
HARLOW, W. M., and HARRAR, E. S. Textbook of dendrology. Ed. 3. New York, McGraw-Hill, 1950. 555 p. $5.00. 454 H22T
HAWLEY, R. C., and STICKEL, P. W. Forest protection. Ed. 2. New York, Wiley, 1948. 355 p. $4.50. 99.5 H31
HAWLEY, R. C. The practice of silviculture. Ed. 5. New York, Wiley, 1946. 354 p. $4.00. 99.45 H31
KITTREDGE, J. Forest influences. New York, McGraw-Hill, 1948. 394 p. $4.50. 99.36 K65
KOROLEFF, A., and FITZWATER, J. A. Managing small woodlands; a guide to good and profitable use of forest land. Washington, Amer. Forestry Assoc., 1947. 72 p. $1.00. 99.55 K842
LILLARD, R. G. The great forest. New York, Knopf, 1947. 399 p. $5.00. 99.04 L62
LUTZ, H. J., and CHANDLER, R. F. Forest soils. New York, Wiley, 1946. 514 p. $5.25. 56.3 L97
MARQUIS, R. W. Economics of private forestry. New York, McGraw-Hill, 1939. 219 p. $3.50. 99.7 M34
MATTHEWS, D. M. Management of American forests. New York, McGraw-Hill, 1935. 495 p. $5.50. 99.55 M43
PANSHIN, A. J., and others. Forest products; their sources, production, and utilization. New York, McGraw-Hill, 1950. 549 p. $6.00. 99.75 P19
   E. S. Harrar, W. J. Baker, and P. B. Proctor, joint authors.

PINCHOT, G. Breaking new ground. New York, Harcourt, Brace, 1947. 522 p. $5.00. 120 P652
PRESTON, J. F. Farm wood crops. New York, McGraw-Hill, 1949. 302 p. $3.75. 99.61 P92
PRESTON, R. J. North American trees. Ames, Iowa State Col. Press, 1948. 371 p. $4.00. 454 P92
RECORD, S. J., and HESS, R. W. Timbers of the New World. New Haven, Yale U. Press, 1943. 640 p. $12.00. 99.79 R24Tn
RODGERS, A. D. Bernhard Edward Fernow; a story of North American forestry. Princeton, Princeton U. Press, 1951. 623 p. $7.50. 120 F392
SOCIETY OF AMERICAN FORESTERS. Fifty years of forestry in the U. S. A. Washington, 1950. 385 p. $4.00. 99.04 So1
SPURR, S. H. Aerial photographs in forestry. New York, Ronald, 1948. 340 p. $6.00. 325.2 Sp9
TIEMANN, H. D. Wood technology; constitution, properties, and uses. Ed. 3. New York, Pitman, 1951. 396 p. $6.00. 99.79 T44
TOUMEY, J. W. Foundations of silviculture upon an ecological basis. Ed. 2, rev. by C. F. Korstian. New York, Wiley, 1947. 468 p. $6.00. 99.45 T64F
TOUMEY, J. W., and Korstian, C. F. Seeding and planting in the practice of forestry. Ed. 3. New York, Wiley, 1942. 520 p. $6.00. 99.47 T64
U. S. DEPT. OF AGRICULTURE. Trees. Yearbook of agriculture, 1949. Washington, U. S. Govt. Print. Off, 1949. 944 p. $2.00. 1 Ag84Y
WACKERMAN, A. E. Harvesting timber crops. New York, McGraw-Hill, 1949. 437 p. $6.00. 99.76 W11
WANGAARD, F. F. Mechanical properties of wood. New York, Wiley, 1950. 377 p. $6.00. 99.79 W11
WESTVELD, R. H. Applied silviculture in the United States. Ed. 2. New York, Wiley, 1949. 567 p. $6.00. 99.45 W52
WESTVELD, R. H., and PECK, R. H. Forestry in farm management. Ed. 2. New York, Wiley, 1951. 340 p. $5.00. 99.55 W52
WILDE, S. A. Forest soils and forest growth. Waltham, Chronica Bot., 1946. 241 p. (Plant Science Books, n. s., v. 18). $5.00. 56.3 W64F

PLANT GROWTH AND GROWTH SUBSTANCES

AVERY, G. S., and JOHNSON, E. B. Hormones and horticulture; the use of special chemicals in the control of plant growth. New York, McGraw-Hill, 1947. 326 p. $4.50. 90.11 Av3
CROCKER, W. Growth of plants; twenty years' research at Boyce Thompson Institute. New York, Reinhold, 1948. $10.00. 463.36 C87
MITCHELL, J. W., and MARTH, P. C. Growth regulators for garden, field, and orchard. Chicago, U. Chicago Press, 1947. 129 p. $2.50. 90.11 M69
SKOOG, F., ed. Plant growth substances. Madison, U. Wis. Press, 1951. 476 p. $6.00. 90.11 Sk5

FUNGI AND PLANT DISEASES

BAWDEN, F. C. Plant viruses and virus diseases. Ed. 3, rev. Waltham, Chronica Bot., 1950. 335 p. $6.00. 464.32 B32
BESSEY, E. A. Morphology and taxonomy of fungi. Philadelphia, Blakiston, 1950. 791 p. $7.00. 462 B46Mo
BOYCE, J. S. Forest pathology. Ed. 2. New York, McGraw-Hill, 1948. 550 p. $6.00. 464.07 B69F
CHESTER, K. S. Nature and prevention of plant diseases. Ed. 2. Philadelphia, Blakiston, 1947. 525 p. $5.00. 464 C42
CHRISTENSEN, C. M. The molds and man; an introduction to the fungi. Minneapolis, U. Minn. Press, 1951. 244 p. $4.00. 462 C46M
COOK, M. T. Viruses and virus diseases of plants. Minneapolis, Burgess, 1947. 244 p. $4.00. 464.32 C77
DICKSON, J. G. Diseases of field crops. New York, McGraw-Hill, 1947. 429 p. $5.00. 464.04 D56
DODGE, B. O., and RICKETT, H. W. Diseases and pests of ornamental plants. Rev. ed. New York, Ronald, 1948. 638 p. $6.00. 464.08 D66
ELLIOTT, C. Manual of bacterial plant pathogens. Ed. 2, rev. Waltham, Chronica Bot., 1951. 186 p. $6.00. (Annales Cryptogamici et Phytopathologici, 10). 450 An77
FAWCETT, H. S. Citrus diseases and their control. Ed. 2. New York, McGraw-Hill, 1936. 656 p. $7.50. 464.06 F28
HEALD, F. D. Introduction to plant pathology. Ed. 2. New York, McGraw-Hill, 1945. 603 p. $6.50. 464 H34In
LEACH, J. G. Insect transmission of plant diseases. New York, McGraw-Hill, 1940. 615 p. $7.50. 423 L462

LILLY, V. G., and BARNETT, H. L. Physiology of the fungi. New York, McGraw-Hill, 1951. 464 p. $7.50. 462.8 L62

M/ RTIN, G. W. Outline of the fungi. Dubuque, Brown, 1950. 82 p. $1.00. 462 M363

PYENSON, L. Elements of plant protection. New York, Wiley, 1951. 538 p. $4.96. 464.4 P99

SPRAGUE, R. Diseases of cereals and grasses in North America (fungi, except smuts and rusts). New York, Ronald, 1950. 538 p. $7.00. 462.17 Sp7

WALKER, J. C. Plant pathology, New York, McGraw-Hill 1950. 699 p. $7.50. 464 W15

WESTCOTT, C. Plant disease handbook. New York, Van Nostrand, 1950. 746 p. $7.50. 464 W523

WESTCOTT, C. The plant doctor. Ed. 3, rev. Philadelphia, Lippincott, 1950. 231 p. $3.00. 464.4 W52

WOLF, F. A., and WOLF, F. T. The fungi. New York, Wiley, 1947. 2 v. v. 1, $6.00; v. 2, $6.50. 462 W832

INSECTICIDES AND FUNGICIDES

DE ONG, E. R. Chemistry and uses of insecticides. New York, Reinhold, 1948. 345 p. $6.75. 423 D44C

DETHIER, V. G. Chemical insect attractants and repellents. Philadelphia, Blakiston, 1947. 289 p. $5.00. 423 D484

FREAR, D. E. H. Chemistry of insecticides, fungicides and herbicides. Ed. 2. New York, Van Nostrand, 1948. 417 p. $6.50. 386 F87

HORSFALL, J. G. Fungicides and their action. Waltham, Chronica Bot., 1945. 239 p. $5.00. 450 An77

HOUGH, W. S., and MASON, A. F. Spraying, dusting and fumigating of plants. Rev. ed. New York, Macmillan, 1951. 726 p. $12.50. 464.4 H81

SHEPARD, H. H. Chemistry and action of insecticides. New York, McGraw-Hill, 1951. 504 p. $7.00. 423 Sh4C

INSECTS

BAILEY, S. F., and SMITH, L. M. Handbook of agricultural pest control. New York, Indus. Publications, 1951. 191 p. $3.25. 464.4 B15

BRUES, C. T. Insect dietary; an account of the food habits of insects. Cambridge, Harvard U. Press, 1946. 466 p., illus. $5.00. 422 B835I

BRUES, C. T. Insects and human welfare; an account of the more important relations of insects to the health of man, to agriculture, and to forestry. Rev. ed. Cambridge, Harvard U. Press, 1947. 154 p., illus. $3.00. 423 B832

CHAMBERLIN, W. J. Insects affecting forest products and other materials. Corvallis, OSC Coop. Assoc., 1949. 159 p. $2.75. 423 C352In

CLAUSEN, C. P. Entomophagous insects. Ed. 1. New York, McGraw-Hill, 1940. 688 p. $8.50. 422 C57

COMSTOCK, J. H. An introduction to entomology. Ed. 9, rev. Ithaca, Comstock, 1940. 1064 p. $6.00. 422 C73It

COTTON, R. T. Insect pests of stored grain and grain products, identification, habits, and methods of control. Rev. ed. Minneapolis, Burgess, 1950. 244 p. $3.25. 423 C82

CURRAN, C. H. Insects in your life. New York, Sheridan, 1951. 316 p. $3.50. 422 C93

DOANE, R. W., VAN DYKE, E. C., CHAMBERLIN, W. J., and BURKE, H. E. Forest insects; a textbook for the use of students in forest schools, colleges, and universities, and for forest workers. New York, McGraw-Hill, 1936. 463 p. $6.00. 423 D65F

EBELING, W. Subtropical entomology. San Francisco, Lithotype Process Co., 1950. 747 p. $7.50. 423 Eb3S

FERNALD, H. T., and SHEPARD, H. H. Applied entomology; an introductory text-book of insects in their relations to man. Ed. 4. New York, McGraw-Hill, 1942. 400 p. $4.50. 423 F39A

GERTSCH, W. J. American spiders. New York, Van Nostrand, 1949. 285 p. $6.95. 434 G322

GRAHAM, S. A. Principles of forest entomology. Ed. 2. New York, McGraw-Hill, 1939. 410 p. $5.00. 423 G762

HERMS, W. B. Medical entomology with special reference to the health and well-being of man and animals. Ed. 4. New York, Macmillan, 1950. 643 p. $9.00. 422 H422M

HOLLAND, W. J. The butterfly book. Rev. ed. Garden City, Doubleday, 1931. 424 p. $12.50. 430 H71

KOFOID, C. A., ed. Termites and termite control. Ed. 2. Berkeley, U. Calif. Press, 1934. 795 p. $6.50. 432 K822

MATHESON, R. Entomology for introductory courses. Ed. 2. Ithaca, Comstock, 1951. 629 p. $6.00. 422 M42E

MATHESON, R. Handbook of the mosquitoes of North America; their anatomy and biology, how they can be studied and identified, how they carry disease and how they can be controlled. Ed. 2. Ithaca, Comstock, 1944. 314 p. (Handbooks of Amer. Nat. Hist. 5). $4.00. 428 M42

MATHESON, R. Medical entomology. Ed. 2. Ithaca, Comstock, 1950. 612 p. $7.50. 423.2 M42

METCALF, C. L., and FLINT, W. P. Destructive and useful insects, their habits and control. Ed. 3. New York, McGraw-Hill, 1951. 1071 p. $10.00. 423 M563

MICHENER, C. D., and MICHENER, M. H. American social insects: a book about bees, ants, wasps, and termites. New York, Van Nostrand, 1951. 267 p. $6.00. 422 M583

PAINTER, R. H. Insect resistance in crop plants. New York, Macmillan, 1951. 520 p. $3.50. 423 P16

PEAIRS, L. M. Insect pests of farm, garden and orchard. Ed. 4. New York, Wiley, 1941. 549 p. $5.00. 423 Sa5I

PYENSON, L. Pest control in the home garden. New York, Macmillan, 1945. 198 p. $2.75. 423 P99

SNYDER, T. E. Our enemy the termite. Rev. ed. Ithaca, Comstock, 1948. 257 p. $3.50. 432 Sn9

STEINHAUS, E. A. Principles of insect pathology. New York, McGraw-Hill, 1949. 757 p. $9.00. 422 St3P

SWAIN, R. B. The insect guide, orders and major families of North American insects. Garden City, Doubleday, 1948. 261 p., illus. $3.00. 422.1 Sw1

WEST, L. S. The housefly; its natural history, medical importance and control. Ithaca, Comstock, 1951. 584 p. $7.50. 428 W522

BEES

DADANT, C. P., DADANT, J. C., and DADANT, M. G., eds. First lessons in beekeeping. Rev. ed. Hamilton, Amer. Bee J., 1951. 127 p. $1.00. 424 D12Fi

GROUT, R. A., ed. The hive and the honey bee; a new book on beekeeping to succeed the book "Langstroth on the Hive and the honey bee." Hamilton, Amer. Bee J., 1949. 652 p. $4.00. 424 G912

LAIDLAW, H. H., Jr., and ECKERT, J. E. Queen rearing. Hamilton, Amer. Bee J., 1950. 147 p. $2.50. 424 L14

NAILE, F. The life of Langstroth. Ithaca, Cornell U. Press, 1942. 215 p. $2.50. 120 L26

ONSTOTT, K. Beekeeping as a hobby. New York, Harper, 1941. 137 p. $2.00. 424 On7

PEASE, C. H. Backlot beekeeping [the little book for little beekeepers] Canaan, Conn., The author, 1949. 110 p. $2.00. 424 P32

PELLETT, F. C. American honey plants; together with those which are of special value to the beekeeper as sources of pollen. Ed. 4. New York, Orange Judd, 1947. 467 p., illus. $6.00. 424 P36A

PELLETT, F. C. A living from bees. New York, Orange Judd, 1946. 335 p. $3.00. 525 P36L

PHILLIPS, E. F. Beekeeping. Rev. ed. New York, Macmillan, 1928. 490 p. $4.50. 424 P43B

ROOT, A. I., and others. The ABC and XYZ of bee culture; an encyclopedia pertaining to scientific and practical culture of bees. Rev. by E. R. Root and H. H. Root. Medina, The authors, 1950. 703 p. $3.95. 424 R67A

ROOT, H. H. Beeswax; its properties, testing, production, and applications. Brooklyn, N. Y., Chemical Pub. Co, 1951. 154 p. $4.75. 424 R673

SMITH, J. Better queens. Ft. Meyers, The author, 1949. 100 p. $4.00. 424 Sm6B

TEALE, E. W. The golden throng; a book about bees. New York, Dodd, Mead, 1940. 208 p. $5.00. 426 T22

ANIMAL HUSBANDRY

ANDERSON, A. L. Introductory animal husbandry. Rev. ed New York, Macmillan, 1951. 701 p. $6.00. 40 An22

ASHBROOK, F. G. Raising small animals for pleasure and profit. New York, Van Nostrand, 1951. 260 p. $4.00. 31.3 As3

BRIGGS, H. M. Modern breeds of livestock. New York, Macmillan, 1949. 772 p. $5.50. 40 B76

CHAPMAN, P. W., and DINSMORE, W. Livestock farming. Rev. ed. Atlanta, Smith, 1947. 616 p. $2.96. 40 C362

-- 8 --

CLAWSON, M. Western range livestock industry. New York, McGraw-Hill, 1950. 401 p. $5.00. 40 C57

ENSMINGER, M. E. Animal science. Ed. 2. Danville, Interstate, 1951. 1096 p. $7.00. 40 En7

NORDBY, J. E., BEESON, W. M., and FOURT, D. L. Livestock judging handbook. [Ed. 6] Danville, Interstate, 1951. 392 p. $3.75. 40 N75

PETERS, W. H. Livestock production. New York, McGraw-Hill, 1942. 450 p. $4.50. 40 P44

PETERS, W. H., and DEYOE, G. P. Raising livestock. New York, McGraw-Hill, 1946. 519 p. $4.50. 40 P44R

SAUNDERSON, M. H. Western stock ranching. Minneapolis, U. Minn. Press, 1950. 247 p. $5.00. 60.1 Sa8

SMITH, W. W. Elements of livestock judging. Rev. ed. Philadelphia, Lippincott, 1941. 294 p. $3.00. 40 Sm6

VAUGHAN, H. W. Breeds of livestock in America. Columbus, Long's Col. Book, 1950. 780 p. $4.75. 40 V46B

WHITNEY, L. F. Complete book of home pet care. Garden City, N. Y., Doubleday, 1950. 552 p. $4.95. ·41 W61C

Animal Anatomy and Physiology

BENSLEY, B. A. Practical anatomy of the rabbit; an elementary text-book of the rabbit; an elementary laboratory text-book in mammalian anatomy. Ed. 8, rev. by E. H. Craigie. Philadelphia, Blakiston, 1948. 319 p. $4.25. 444 B44

COWDRY, E. V. A textbook of histology; functional significance of cells and intercellular substance. Ed. 4. Philadelphia, Lea & Febiger, 1950. 640 p. $8.50. 442 C834T

DAVISON, A. Mammalian anatomy with special reference to the cat. Ed. 7. rev. by F. A. Stronsten. Philadelphia, Blakiston, 1947. 349 p. $4.50. 444 D29

HOLSTAD, G. E. The fetal pig; an introduction to the anatomy of the fetal pig. Minneapolis, Burgess, 1950. 32 p. $1.65. 444 H742

JONES, R. M., ed. McClung's handbook of microscopical technique for workers in animal and plant tissues. Ed. 3. New York, Hoeber, 1950. 790 p. $12.50. 440 J72

LYON, M. The dog in action; a study of anatomy and locomotion as applying to all breeds. New York, Orange Judd, 1950. 288 p. $4.50. 444 L99

PATTEN, B. M. Early embryology of the chick. 4th ed. Philadelphia, Blakiston, 1951. 244 p. $3.50. 442 P27

PATTEN, B. M. Embryology of the pig. Ed. 3. Philadelphia, Blakiston, 1948. 352 p. $3.75. 442 P27E

PROSSER, C. L., ed. Comparative animal physiology. Philadelphia, Saunders, 1950. 888 p. $12.50. 444 P943

QUIRING, D. P. Functional anatomy of the vertebrates. New York, McGraw-Hill, 1950. 624 p. $5.50. 444 Q42

ROMANOFF, A. L., and ROMANOFF, A. J. The avian egg. New York, Wiley, 1949. 918 p. $16.00. 413 R66

SISSON, S. The anatomy of the domestic animals. Ed. 3. rev. by J. D. Grossman. Philadelphia, Saunders, 1938. 972 p. $14.50. 41 Si82

TAYLOR, W. T., and WEBER, R. J. Functional mammalian anatomy, with special reference to the cat. N w York, Van Nostrand, 1951. 575 p. $7.25. 444 T21

Animal Diseases and Parasites

AMERICAN ANIMAL HOSPITAL ASSOCIATION. Planning your animal hospital. Skokie, The author, 1950. 155 p. $3.50. 41 Am36

BARGER, E. H., and CARD, L. E. Diseases and parasites of poultry. Ed. 4, rev. Philadelphia, Lea & Febiger, 1949. 400 p. $4.00. 41 B233

BARON, A. L. Handbook of antibiotics. New York, Reinhold, 1950. 303 p. $6.50. 448.2 B26

BENBROOK, E. A. List of parasites of domesticated animals in North America. Minneapolis, Burgess, 1946. 53 p. $1.25. 436 B433

BENBROOK, E. A., and SLOSS, M. W. Manual of veterinary clinical parasitology. Ames, Iowa State Col. Press, 1948. 187 p. $4.50. 436 B433V

BIESTER, H. E., and SCHWARTE, L. H., ed. Diseases of poultry. Ed. 2. Ames, Iowa State Col. Press, 1948. 1154 p. $10.50. 41 B475

BRUMLEY, O. V. A text-book of the diseases of the small domestic animals. Ed. 4. Philadelphia, Lea & Febiger, 1943. 422 p. $5.00. 41 B836T

CHANDLER, A. C. Introduction to parasitology; with special references to the parasites of man. Ed. 8. New York, Wiley, 1949. 756 p. $6.00. 448 C362 Includes parasites of domestic animals.

COFFIN, D. L. Manual of veterinary clinical pathology. Rev. Ithaca, Comstock, 1945. 263 p. $4.00. 41 C65

CONN, G. H. Practical veterinarian. Ed. 2. Columbia, Mo. Livestock Serv., 1949. 192 p. $2.50. 41 C763

CONN, G. H. Some common diseases of cattle. New York, Orange Judd, 1942. 176 p. $1.75. 41 C763S

DORLAND, W. A. N. The American illustrated medical dictionary. Ed. 21. Philadelphia, Saunders, 1947. 1660 p. $8.00; Thumb-indexed $8.50. 448 D73

DYKSTRA, R. R. Animal sanitation and disease control. Rev. ed. Danville, Interstate, 1949. 808 p. $3.50. 41 D99

FRANK, E. R. Veterinary surgery notes. Rev. ed. Minneapolis, Burgess, 1947. 272 p. $5.00. 41 F855

GARBUTT, R. J. Diseases and surgery of the dog. New York, Orange Judd, 1938. 332 p. $4.00. 41 G162

GUARD, W. F. Surgical principles and technics. Columbus, Ohio, The author, 1951. 186 p. $5.50. 41 G934S

HADLEY, F. B. Principles of veterinary science. Ed. 4. Philadelphia, Saunders, 1949. 521 p. $5.00. 41 H117

HAGAN, W. A., and BRUNER, D. W. The infectious diseases of domestic animals. Ed. 2. Ithaca, Comstock, 1951. 920 p. $8.00. 41 H123I

HEGNER, R., and others. Parasitology, with special reference to man and the domesticated animals. New York, Appleton-Century-Crofts, 1938. 812 p. $7.00. 436 H364A
   F. M. Root, D. L. Augustine, and C. G. Huff, joint authors.

HOSKINS, H. P., and LECROIX, J. V., ed. Canine surgery; a text and reference work. Evanston, North Amer. Vet., 1949. 565 p. $12.00. 41 H79

LEAHY, J. R., and BARROW, P. Restraint of animals. Ithaca, The authors, 1951. 234 p. $3.50. 41 L47

LITTLE, R. B., and PLASTRIDGE, W. N., ed. Bovine mastitis; a symposium. New York, McGraw-Hill, 1946. 546 p. $7.00. 41 L722

MERCHANT, I. A. An outline of the infectious diseases of domestic animals. Minneapolis, Burgess, 1951. 360 p. $5.00. 41 M530

MILKS, H. J. Practical veterinary pharmacology, materia medica and therapeutics; with a chapter on biological therapeutics by A. Zeissig. Ed. 6. Chicago, Eger, 1949. 720 p. $10.00. 41 M593

MORGAN, B. B. Bovine trichomoniasis. Rev. ed. Minneapolis, Burgess, 1946. 180 p. $3.25. 41 M823

MORGAN, B. B., and HAWKINS, P. A. Veterinary helminthology. Minneapolis, Burgess, 1949. 399 p. $6.00. 436 M822 ·

MORGAN, B. B., and HAWKINS, P. A. Veterinary protozoology. Minneapolis, Burgess, 1948. 195 p. $4.00. 439 M82

RUNNELLS, R. A. Animal pathology. Ed. 4. Ames, Iowa State Col. Press, 1946. 639 p. $7.00. 41 R873

SCHNELLE, G. B. Radiology in small animal practice; a text on applied radiography and diagnosis, with a section on radiotherapy, by M. Thom. Ed. 2. Evanston, N. Amer. Vet., 1950. 365 p. $8.00. 41 Sch55

STAMM, G. W. Veterinary guide for farmers; ed. by D. S. Burch. [Ed. 2] Chicago, Windsor Press, 1951. 384 p. $3.50. 41 St29

UDALL, D. H. Practice of veterinary medicine. Ed. 5. Ithaca, Udall, 1947. 751 p. $7.50. 41 Ud1P

U. S. DEPT. OF AGRICULTURE. Keeping livestock healthy. Yearbook of agriculture, 1942. Washington, U. S. Govt. Print. Off., 1942. 1276 p. $2.25. · 1 Ag84Y

VAN ES, L. The principles of animal hygiene and preventive veterinary medicine. New York, Wiley, 1932. 768 p. $7.50. 41 V282

WHITE, G. R. Animal castration; a textbook for the use of teachers, students and practitioners. Ed. 3, rev. Nashville, The author, 1947. 287 p. $7.50. 41 W583A

WILLIAMS, W. L. The diseases of the genital organs of domestic animals. Ed. 3, 3rd printing with brief additions by M. G. Fincher. Worcester, Plimpton, 1951[1943] 641 p. $10.80. 41 W672D

WILLIAMS, W. L. Veterinary obstetrics. Reprinted with additions and deletions covering advances in recent

years by S. J. Roberts. Worcester, Plimpton, 1951.
$8.10. 41 W672V

Feeding of Animals

BULL, S., and CARROLL, W. E. Principles of feeding
farm animals. Rev. ed. Danville, Interstate, 1949,
400 p. $3.25. 389.7 B87
MAYNARD, L. A. Animal nutrition. Ed. 3. New York,
McGraw-Hill, 1951. 474 p. $5.50. 389.7 M45
MORRISON, F. B. Feeds and feeding; a handbook for the
student and stockman. Ed. 21. Ithaca, Morrison Pub.
Co., 1948. 1207 p. $7.00. 389.7 M833
MORRISON, F. B. Feeds and feeding abridged; the essentials of the feeding, care and management of farm
animals, including poultry. Ed. 8, adapted and condensed from Feeds and feeding (21st. ed.). Ithaca,
Morrison Pub. Co., 1949. 630 p. $3.50.
389.7 M833A
NATIONAL RESEARCH COUNCIL. COMMITTEE ON AN-
IMAL NUTRITION. Recommended nutrient allow-
ances for domestic animals. Washington, The author,
1945-1949. 6 v., $.50 each. 389.7 N2122
    1. Poultry, 18 p.; 2. Swine, 11 p; 3. Dairy cattle,
    21 p.; 4. Beef cattle, 32 p.; 5. Sheep, 20 p.; 6. Horses,
    29 p.
SCHNEIDER, B. H. Feeds of the world, their digestibility
and composition. Morgantown, W. Va. U. Bookstore,
1947. 299 p. $3.00. 241 Sch54
SHERWOOD, R. M. The feed mixers' handbook. Danville, Interstate, 1951. 192 p. $2.50. 389.7 Sh5

Beef Cattle

BAKER, E. T. The cow owner's handbook. New York,
Prentice-Hall, 1951. 213 p. $2.95. 43 B172
ENSMINGER, M. E. Beef cattle husbandry. Danville, In-
terstate, 1951. 381 p. $3.50. 43 En7
HULTZ, F. S. Range beef production in the seventeen
western states. New York, Wiley, 1930. 208 p.
$3.25. 43 H872
JUERGENSON, E. M. Approved practices in beef cattle
production. Danville, Interstate, 1951. 246 p. $2.10.
43 J93
SNAPP, R. R. Beef cattle; their feeding and management
in the Corn Belt States. Ed. 3. New York, Wiley,
1939. 550.p. 43 Sn1
WIDMEN, J. Practical beef production. New York,
Scribner, 1946. 101 p. $3.00. 43 W63
WILLIAMS, D. W. Beef cattle production in the South.
Danville, Interstate, 1950. 450 p. $3.00. 43 W67

Dogs and Cats

AMERICAN KENNEL CLUB. The complete dog book.
New rev. ed. Garden City, Garden City Pub. Co.,
1951. 753 p. $2.49. 48 Am3?C
BLACKISTON, E. Teaching your dog obedience. New
York, Crown Pub., 1950. 154 p. $2.95. 48 B56
BRYANT, D. The care and handling of cats; a manual for
modern cat owners. Rev. ed. New York, Washburn,
1949. 226 p., illus. $2.75. 48 B84C
CONNETT, E. V., ed. American sporting dogs. New
York, Van Nostrand, 1948. 549 p. $5.00. 48 C762
DAVIS, H. P., ed. The modern dog encyclopedia. New
York, Stackpole & Heck, 1949. 626 p. $10.00.
48 D29W
FAIRCHILD, L. H., and FAIRCHILD, H. G. Cats and all
about them. Rev. ed. New York, Orange Judd, 1947.
243 p. $2.50. 48 F16
HARBISON, C. E. Our dogs; a text book on the feeding,
training and care of all breeds. Rev. New York,
Orange Judd, 1949. 324 p. $4.00. 48 H21
HICKEY, J. H., and BEACH, P. A. Know your cat. New
York, Harper, 1946. 251 p. $2.75. 48 H52
HICKEY, J. H., and BEACH, P. A. Know your dog. New
York, Harper, 1947. 337 p. $3.00. 48 H52K
MCCAY, C. M. Nutrition of the dog. Ed. 2. Ithaca, Com-
stock, 1949. 337 p. $3.50. 389.7 M122N
MELLEN, I. M. A practical cat book for amateurs and
professionals. New York, Scribner, 1939. 230 p.
$3.50. 48 M48
NORTON, M. A. Cats; care, training, feeding, breeding,
exhibiting. New York, Pitman, 1949. 142 p. $2.75.
48 N82
ONSTOTT, K. The art of breeding better dogs. Washing-
ton, Denlinger's, 1946. 231 p. $4.50. 48 On7
PEAKE, H. C. Practical dog breeding. New York, Macmillan, 1945. 145 p. $1.95. 48 P312
RINE, J. Z. The dog owner's manual. Rev. ed. New

York, Tudor, 1950. 455 p. $3.00. 48 R47D
TAYNTON, M. Successful kennel management; how to
make money breeding and boarding dogs. New York,
McGraw-Hill, 1951. 213 p. $4.00. 48 T21
TOSSUTTI, H. Companion dog training; a practical man-
ual on systematic obedience, dog training in word and
picture. New York, Orange Judd, 1948. 272 p.
$3.00. 48 T63
WHITNEY, L. F. Feeding our dogs. New York, Van
Nostrand, 1949. 243 p. $3.50. 389.7 W61
WHITNEY, L. F. How to breed dogs, a popular exposi-
tion of the scientific principles underlying reproduc-
tion and heredity in dogs, with special reference to
their practical application. Rev. ed. New York,
Orange Judd, 1947. 418 p. $4.50. 48 W61

Fur Farming

ADAMS, L. H. Mink raising; a book of practical informa-
tion about raising mink, marten and fisher. Ed. 4.
Columbus, Ohio, Fur Fish Game, 1935. 225 p.
$1.50. 412.62 Ad1
ASHBROOK, F. G. Fur farming for profit. Rev. and
reset. New York, Orange Judd, 1948. 429 p. $5.00.
412.62 As3
BACHRACH, M. Fur; a practical treatise. Rev. ed.
New York, Prentice-Hall, 1946. 672 p. $7.50; Text
ed. $5.65. 412.62 B12
HOUSTON, J. W. Chinchilla care. Gardena, Calif. Allied
Fur Indus., 1951. 148 p. $3.00. 412.62 H81
KING, A. W. Genetics of mink; a handbook for the student
and rancher. Duluth, Internatl. Pub. Co., 1951.
183 p. $6.00. 412.62 K458
SHACKELFORD, R. M. Genetics of ranch mink. New
York, Pilsbury, 1950. 91 p. $5.00. 412.62 Sh1

Horses

BROWN, W. R. Horse of the desert. New York, Mac-
millan, 1947. 218 p. $12.00. 42 B812
CONN, G. H. The practical horse keeper. Rev. ed. New
York, Orange Judd, 1950. 284 p. $3.50. 42 C76
DENHARDT, R. M. The horse of the Americas. Norman,
U. Okla. Press, 1947. 286 p. $5.00. 42 D41H
ENSMINGER, M. E. Horse husbandry. Danville, Inter-
state, 1951. 336 p. $3.50. 42 En7
GORMAN, J. A. The western horse; its types and train-
ing. Danville, Interstate, 1949. 396 p. $3.50.
42 G68
ROOKS, C. F. Light horses. Chicago, Ziff-Davis, 1946.
159 p. $2.75. 42 R67
SELF, M. C. The horseman's encyclopedia. New York,
Barnes, 1946. 519 p. $5.00. 42 Se4H
TAYLOR, L. The horse America made, the story and
analysis of the world's greatest saddle horse, and a
simple, explicit guide for training, riding and rearing.
Louisville, Amer. Saddle Horse Breeders Assoc.,
1944. 243 p. $4.00. 42 T212
VAN SINDEREN, A. Behind the scenes at a horse show.
New York, Scribner, 1948. 136 p. $3.75. 42 V36
WALL, J. F. A horseman's handbook of practical breed-
ing. Ed. 3, rev. Washington, Amer. Remount Assoc.,
1950. 412 p. $5.75. 42 W152H
WIDMER, J. Practical horse breeding and training. New
York, Scribner, 1944. 114 p. $3.50. 42 W63
WILLIAMSON, C. O. Breaking and training the stock
horse. New Plymouth, The author, 1950. 89 p.
$7.50. 42 W67

Laboratory Animals, Small

DEICKE, E. F. Cavies for pleasure and profit. Ed. 4.
Lombard, 1944. 119 p. $2.00. 48 D36
FARRIS, E. J., ed. The care and breeding of laboratory
animals. New York, Wiley, 1950. 515 p. $8.00.
411 F24
GALE, L. C. The golden hamster manual. Concordia,
Kans., The author, 1949. 73 p. $1.50. 412.7 G13G
GRIFFITH, J. Q., and FARRIS, E. J., ed. The rat in lab-
oratory investigation; by a staff of twenty-nine con-
tributors. Ed. 2. Philadelphia, Lippincott, 1949.
541 p. $15.00. 412.7 G873
REYNOLDS, H. W. Golden hamsters. [Silver Spring, Md.]
Denlinger, 1950. 28 p. $.25. 412.7 R33
ZIM, H. S. Golden hamsters. N. Y., Morrow, 1951. 63 p.
$2.00. 412.7 Z62

Poultry

AMERICAN POULTRY ASSOCIATION. The American

standard of perfection, illustrated. A complete description of all recognized varieties of fowls. Davenport, The author, 1947. 492 p. $3.50. 47.9 Am35A Supplement of 7 pages issued in 1947.

CARD, L. E., and HENDERSON, M. Farm poultry production. Ed. 4. Danville, Interstate, 1948. 230 p. $2.50. 47 C173

CHARLES, T. B., and STUART, H. O. Commercial poultry farming. Ed. by L. L. Scranton. Ed. 7. Danville, Interstate, 1949. 540 p. $4.75. 47 C382

COOK, G. C. Approved practices in poultry production. Danville, Interstate, 1945. 187 p. $1.50. 47 C772

COOPER, J. B. Poultry for home and market. Atlanta, Smith, 1950. 487 p. $3.39. 47 C782

EWING, W, R. Poultry nutrition;...text and reference book for instructors, students and all persons interested in poultry feeds and feeding. Ed. 4. South Pasadena, The author, 1951. 1518 p. $12.50. 47 Ew5

FLOREA, J. H. ABC of poultry raising; a complete guide for the beginner or expert. New York, Greenberg, 1944. 206 p. $2.50. 47 F66

GIBBS, C. S. A guide to sexing chicks. New York, Orange Judd, 1943. 63 p. $2.00. 47 G352

GREENBERG, D. B. Raising game birds in captivity. New York, Van Nostrand, 1949. 224 p. $5.95. 47.5 G82

HAMILTON, S. W. Profitable turkey management. 8th ed Cayuga, Beacon Milling Co., 1951. 128 p. $1.25. 47.3 H18

HARTMAN, R. C., and VICKERS, G. S. Hatchery management. Rev. New York, Orange Judd, 1951. 404 p. $4.00. 47 H25

HARTMAN, R. C. Keeping chickens in cages; a description of the outdoor individual cage system of poultry management as developed mainly in southern California. Redlands, Calif., The Author, 1950. 181 p. $3.25. 47 H25K

HEUSER, G. F. Feeding poultry. New York, Wiley, 1946. 543 p. $5.50. 47 H48F

HOFFMANN, E., and GWIN, J. M. Successful broiler growing. Ed. 2. Mount Morris, Watt, 1951. 256 p. $3.50. 47 H674

HUNTER, J. M., and SCHOLES, J. C. Profitable duck management. Ed. 8. Cayuga, Beacon Milling Co., 1950. 76 p. $.75. 47.1 H91P

HURD, L. M. Modern poultry farming. New York, Macmillan, 1944. 599 p. $4.00. 47 H93

HUTT, F. B. Genetics of the fowl. New York, McGraw-Hill, 1949. 590 p. $6.50. 47 H97

IVES, P. Domestic geese and ducks; a complete and authentic handbook and guide for breeders, growers and admirers of domestic geese and ducks. New York, Orange Judd, 1947. 372 p. $3.50. 47.1 Iv3

JULL, M. A. Poultry breeding. Ed. 2. New York, Wiley, 1940. 484 p. $5.00. 47 J94Po

JULL, M. A. Poultry husbandry. Ed. 3. New York, McGraw-Hill, 1951. 526 p. $6.00. 47 J94P

JULL, M. A. Raising turkeys, ducks, geese, game birds. New York, McGraw-Hill, 1947. 467 p. $4.00. 47 J94R

JULL, M. A. Successful poultry management. Ed. 2. New York, McGraw-Hill, 1951. 447 p. $5.00. 47 J94s

KAUPP, B. F., and SURFACE, R. C. Poultry sanitation and disease control; the complete guide to sanitation and treatment of disease. Minneapolis, The authors, 1950. 493 p. $4.50. 41 K163P

KING, D. F., and CHESNUTT, S. L. Poultry production in the South. Ed. by M. D. Mobley. Danville, Interstate, 1943. 243 p. $2.80. 47 K58

KLEIN, G. T. Starting right with poultry. Ed. by E. Robinson. New York, Macmillan, 1950[1947] 177 p. $1.75. 47 K672S

KLEIN, G. T. Starting right with turkeys. Ed. by E. Robinson. New York, Macmillan, 1950[1946] 129 p. $1.49. 47.3 K67

LEE, C. E. Profitable poultry management. Ed. 19. Cayuga, Beacon Milling Co., 1951. 272 p. $1.80. 47 L51

LEVI, W. M. Making pigeons pay; a manual of practical information on the management, selection, breeding, feeding, and marketing of pigeons. New York, Orange Judd, 1946. 263 p. $3.00. 47.2 L57M

LIPPINCOTT, W. A. Poultry production. Ed. 7, rev. by L. E. Card. Philadelphia, Lea & Febiger, 1946. 440 p. $4.00. 47 L66

MARSDEN, S. J., and MARTIN, J. H. Turkey management. Ed. 5. Danville, Interstate, 1949. 774 p., illus $5.50. 47.3 M35

NAETHER, C. A. The book of the pigeon. Ed. 3. Philadelphia, McKay, 1944. 242 p. $3.00. 47.2 N12

NAETHER, C. A. The book of the racing pigeon. New York, McKay, 1950. 244 p. $3.50. 47.2 N12B

PAYNE, L. F., and AVERY, T. B. International poultry guide for flock selection; covering the more popular breeds and varieties of chickens and turkeys. Ed. 2. Kansas City, Internatl. Baby Chick Assoc., 1950. 247 p. $3.75. 47 P292

RAE, T. Profitable game bird management. Ed. 7. Cayuga, Beacon Milling Co., 1950. 80 p. $1.00. 47.5 R12

RICE, J. E., and BOTSFORD, H. E. Practical poultry management. Ed. 5. New York, Wiley, 1949. 614 p. $3.96. 47 R362

ROBERTS, H. A., and PLATT, C. S. Commercial poultry raising. Philadelphia, McKay, 1947. 554 p. $3.50. 47 R54

SEIDEN, R., ed. Poultry handbook; an encyclopedia for good management of all poultry breeds. New ed. New York, Van Nostrand, 1949. 410 p. $4.95. 47 Se4

TAYLOR, L. W., ed. Fertility and hatchability of chicken and turkey eggs. New York, Wiley, 1949. 423 p. $5.50. 47 T212F

TITUS, H. W. The scientific feeding of chickens. Ed. 2. Danville, Interstate, 1949. 253 p. $2.80. 47 T54

WINTER, A. R., and FUNK, E. M. Poultry; science and practice. Ed. by R. W. Gregory. Ed. 3. Philadelphia Lippincott, 1951. 662 p. $5.50. 47 W732

ZIM, H. S. Homing pigeons. New York, Morrow, 1949. 62 p. $2.00. 47.2 Z6

Rabbits

AMERICAN RABBIT AND CAVY BREEDERS ASSOCIATION, INC. Guide book and standard, 1950-53. Pittsburgh, The author, 1950. 320 p. Free with membership ($3.00). 40.2 Am35

ASHBROOK, F. G. How to raise rabbits for food and fur. New York, Orange Judd, 1943. 256 p. $3.00. 40.2 As3

FEHR, J. C., ed. Rabbit judging manual. Indianapolis, The editor, 1944. 60 p. $1.00. 40.2 F32

GILBERT, A. T. American Angora handbook. Ed. 5. East Haven, Gilcrest Angora Center, 1942. 112 p. $1.50. 40.2 G37

MEEK, M. W. Rabbit raising for profit. New York, Greenberg, 1947. 356 p. $4.00. 40.2 M47

Sheep and Goats

BAKER, E. T. Management and feeding of sheep; a practical treatise on the selection, care, and breeding, including chapters on the diseases and ailments of sheep. New York, Orange Judd, 1947. 396 p. $4.00. 45 B17

ENSMINGER, M. E. Sheep husbandry. Danville, Interstate, 1952. 404 p. $3.00. 45 En7

HORLACHER, L. J., and HAMMONDS, C. Sheep. Ed. 3. Danville, Interstate, 1950. 348 p. $2.50. 45 H78S

HULTZ. F. S., and HILL, J. A. Range sheep and wool in the seventeen Western States. New York, Wiley, 1931. 374 p. $4.00. 45 H87

KAMMLADE, W. G. Sheep science. Ed. by R. W. Gregory. Philadelphia, Lippincott, 1947. 534 p. $5.50. 45 K12

LEACH, C. A. Aids to goatkeeping. Ed. 5. Columbia, Dairy Goat J., 1946. 143 p. $3.50. 40.1 L46

LEACH, C. E. Dairy goat husbandry and disease control. Columbia, Mo., Journal Press, 1950. 164 p. $3.50. 41 L46

LEGGETT, W. F. The story of wool. Brooklyn, Chem. Pub. Co., 1947. 304 p. $5.00. 45 L524

TEWALT, W. L. Improved milk goats; a guide for breeders, dairymen, and exhibitors. New York, Orange Judd, 1942. 145 p. $1.50. 40.1 T31

VON BERGEN, W., and MAUERSBERGER, H. R. American wool handbook; a practical text and reference book for the entire wool industry. Ed. 2, enl. New York, Textile Book. Pub., 1948. 1055 p. $8.80. 304 V89

WALSH, H. Starting right with milk goats. Ed. by E. Robinson. New York, Macmillan, 1950[1947] 138 p. $1.49. 40.1 W16

Swine

ANDERSON, A. L. Swine management, including feeding and breeding. Ed. by R. W. Gregory. Philadelphia, Lippincott, 1950. 531 p. $3.40. 46 An2S

CARROLL, W. E., and KRIDER, J. L. Swine production. New York, McGraw-Hill. 1950. 498 p. $5.50.

46 C23S
COOK, G. C. Approved practices in swine production. Danville, Interstate, 1948. 209 p. $2.10. 46 C772

SMITH, W. W. Pork production; with a chapter on the prevention of hog diseases, by R. A. Craig. Rev. ed. New York, Macmillan, 1937. $5.00. 46 Sm6

SOUTHWELL, B. L., WHEELER, J. T., and DUNCAN, A. O. Swine production in the South. Danville, Interstate, 1940. 307 p. $3.00. 46 So8

DAIRYING

ADAMS, H. S. Milk and food sanitation practice. New York, Commonwealth Fund, 1947. 311 p. $3.25. 389 Ad12

AMERICAN PUBLIC HEALTH ASSOCIATION. Standard methods for the examination of dairy products. Ed. 9. New York, The author, 1948. 373 p. $4.00. 448.2 Am3

ECKLES, C. H. Dairy cattle and milk production. Ed. 4, rev. by E. L. Anthony. New York, Macmillan, 1950. 560 p. $5.00. 43 Ec5

ECKLES, C. H., COMBS, W. B., and MACY, H. Milk and milk products. Ed. 4. New York, McGraw-Hill, 1951. 454 p. $5.00. 44 Ec5M

ESPE, D. L. Secretion of milk. Ed. 3. Ames, Iowa State Col. Press, 1946. 320 p. $3.75. 44 Es6

FARRALL, A. W. Dairy engineering. New York, Wiley, 1942. 405 p. $5.50. 44 F242

FOUTS, E. L., and FREEMAN, T. R. Dairy manufacturing processes; a handbook for dairy plant workers and short course students. New York, Wiley, 1948. 237 p. $3.50. 44 F822

FRASER, W. J. Dairy profit. Rev. ed. Danville, Interstate, 1949. 316 p. $2.25. 44 F862

GILMORE, L. D. Dairy cattle breeding. New York, Lippincott, 1951. 604 p. $5.50.

HERRINGTON, B. L. Milk and milk processing. New York, McGraw-Hill, 1948. 343 p. $4.00. 44 H433

HUNZIKER, O. F. Butter industry. Ed. 3. LaGrange, Ill., The author, 1940. 821 p. $8.50. 44 H92B

HUNZIKER, O. F. Condensed milk and milk powder. Ed. 7, completely rev. LaGrange, Ill., 1949. 585 p., illus. $7.00. 44 H92

INGHAM, R. W. Grass silage and dairying. New Brunswick, Rutgers U. Press, 1949. 88 p. $1.50. 389.7 In4

JUDKINS, H. F. Principles of dairying; testing and manufactures. Ed. 3 by M. J. Mack. New York, Wiley, 1941. 315 p. $3.75. 44 J91

KELLY, E., and CLEMENT, C. E. Market milk. Ed. 2. New York, Wiley, 1931. 489 p. $5.50. 44 K29

LASCELLES, H. R. Western dairying. Danville, Interstate, 1951. 280 p. $3.00. 44 L334

MILK INDUSTRY FOUNDATION. Laboratory manual; methods of analysis of milk and its products. Ed. 2. Washington, The author, 1949. 629 p. $15.00. 44 M592L

NELSON, J. A., and TROUT, G. M. Judging dairy products. Ed. 2. Milwaukee, Olsen, 1948. 494 p. $6.50. 44 N33

NEVENS, W. B. Principles of milk production. Ed. 2. New York, McGraw-Hill, 1951. 443 p. $5.00. 44 N412

NEWMAN, P. E. Profitable dairy management. Ed. 8. Cayuga, Beacon Milling Co., 1951. 128 p. $1.25. 43 N462

OLSON, T. M. Elements of dairying. Rev. ed. New York, Macmillan, 1950. 708 p. $5.50. 44 OL82

PETERSEN, W. E. Dairy science; its principles and practice. Ed. 2. Philadelphia, Lippincott, 1950. 695 p. $5.50. 44 P444

ROADHOUSE, C. L., and HENDERSON, J. L. The market-milk industry. Ed. 2. New York, McGraw-Hill, 1950. 716 p. $7.00. 44 R53

SAMMIS, J. L. Cheese making; a book for practical cheese-makers, factory patrons, agricultural colleges and dairy schools. Ed. 12, rev. Madison, Cheesemaker Book, 1948. 333 p. $3.50. 44 D35C

SOMMER, H. H. Theory and practice of ice cream making. Ed. 6. Milwaukee, Olsen Pub. Co., 1951. 723 p. $7.00. 389.2 So52

THOMAS, R. H., REAVES, P. M., and PEGRAM, C. W. Dairy farming in the South. Rev. ed. Danville, Interstate, 1949. 431 p., illus. $3.00. 44 T362

VAN SLYKE, L. L., and PRICE, W. V. Cheese. Rev. & enl. ed. New York, Orange Judd, 1949. 522 p. $4.50. 44 V36C

WHITTIER, E. O., and WEBB, B. H. Byproducts from milk. New York, Reinhold, 1950. 317 p. $6.00. 44 W61

WILSTER, G. H. Practical butter manufacture; a manual for buttermakers. Ed. 7. Corvallis, OSC Coop. Assoc., 1951. 497 p. $5.75. 44 W693

WILSTER, G. H. Practical Cheddar cheese manufacture and cheese technology. Ed. 7. Corvallis, OSC Coop. Assoc., 1951. 515 p. $5.75. 44 W693P

WILSTER, G. H. Testing dairy products and dairy plant sanitation. Ed. 3. Corvallis, OSC Coop. Assoc., 1950. 295 p. $2.50. 44 W693T

SOILS, FERTILIZERS, AND PLANT NUTRITION

AMERICAN SOCIETY OF AGRONOMY. Hunger signs in crops; a symposium prepared by F. E. Bear [and others] Ed. 2. Washington, Natl. Fertilizer Assoc., 1949. 390 p. $4.50. 463.34 Am3

ANDREWS, W. B. The response of crops and soils to fertilizers and manures. State College, Miss., The author, 1947. 459 p. $4.50. 57.07 An2

BAVER, L. D. Soil physics. Ed. 2. New York, Wiley, 1948. 398 p. $4.75. 56.43 B32

BEAR, F. E. Diagnostic techniques for soils and crops. Washington, Amer. Potash Inst., 1948. 308 p. $2.00. 395 B38D

BEAR, F. E. Soils and fertilizers. Ed. 3. New York, Wiley, 1942. 374 p. $3.75. 56.7 B38

BEAUMONT, A. B. Artificial manures: or, The conservation and use of organic matter for soil improvement. New York, Orange Judd, 1943. 155 p. $2.00. 57.4 B38

BEAUMONT, A. B. Garden soils, their use and construction. New York, Orange Judd, 1948. 280 p. $3.50. 56.7 B382

COLLINGS, G. H. Commercial fertilizers, their sources and use. Ed. 4. Philadelphia, Blakiston, 1950[1947] 522 p. $5.00. 57.2 C69

GILMAN, J. C. A manual of soil fungi. Iowa State Col. Press, 1945. 392 p. $5.00. 462 G42

GUSTAFSON, A. F. Handbook of fertilizers: their sources, make-up, effects and use. Ed. 4, rev. New York, Orange Judd, 1945. 172 p. $2.00. 57 G97

GUSTAFSON, A. F. Using and managing soils. New York, McGraw-Hill, 1948. 420 p. $3.00. 56.7 G97U

HOAGLAND, D. R. Lectures on the inorganic nutrition of plants. Waltham, Chronica Botanica, 1944. 226 p. (New Ser. of Plant Sci. Books v. 14). $4.50. 463.34 H65

JENNY, H. Factors of soil formation; a system of quantitative pedology. New York, McGraw-Hill, 1941. 281 p. $4.50. 56.1 J45

JOFFE, J. S. The ABC of soils. New Brunswick, Pedology Pubs., 1949. 383 p. $3.80. 56 J59

JOFFE, J. S. Pedology. With an introduction by C. F. Marbut. Ed. 2. New Brunswick, Pedology Pub., 1949. 662 p. $6.25. 56.1 J59

KELLEY, W. P. Alkali soils; their formation, properties, and reclamation. New York, Reinhold, 1951. 176 p. (American Chemical Society (Monog. 111) $5.00. 56.33 K28

KELLEY, W. P. Cation exchange in soils. New York, Reinhold, 1948. 144 p. (American Chemical Society Monograph Series 109). $4.50. 56.4 K28

KELLOGG, C. E. The soils that support us. New York, Macmillan, 1941. 370 p. $4.50. 56 K29

KRAMER, P. J. Plant and soil water relationships. New York, McGraw-Hill, 1949. 347 p. $4.50. 463.3 K86

LAMBE, T. W. Soil testing for engineers. New York, Wiley, 1951. 165 p. $5.00. 56.43 L17

LAURIE, A., and KIPLINGER, D. C. Soils and fertilizers for greenhouse and garden. New York, De La Mare, 1948. 128 p. $2.50. 57 L37

LYON, T. L., and BUCKMAN, H. O. The nature and properties of soils. Ed. 4. New York, Macmillan, 1947. 499 p. $4.75. 56 L99N

MARSHALL, C. E. Colloid chemistry of the silicate minerals. New York, Academic Press, 1949. 195 p. $5.80. 386 M352

MILLAR, C. E., and TURK, L. M. Fundamentals of soil science. Ed. 2. New York, Wiley, 1951. 510 p. $5.50. 56 M613

PURI, A. N. Soils; their physics and chemistry. New York, Reinhold, 1949. 550 p. $7.00. 56.4 P97

SAUCHELLI, V. Manual on fertilizer manufacture. Baltimore, Davison Chem. Corp., 1946. 126 p. $4.00. 57.2 Sa8

SCHWAB, G. O., FREVERT, R. K., and BARNES, K. K. Manual of soil and water conservation engineering. Dubuque, W. C. Brown, 1950. 222 p. $2.50. 56.7 Sch92

SOWERS, G. B., and SOWERS, G. F. Introductory soil mechanics and foundations. New York, Macmillan,

1951. 284 p. $4.75. 56.43 So92
SPURWAY, C. H. Soil fertility diagnosis and control for
field, garden, and greenhouse soils. East Lansing,
The author, 1949. 176 p. $3.50. 566 Sp9
SUCCESSFUL farming. A better living from your soil;
ed. by Jim Roe and William Raufer. Des Moines,
Meredith, 1949. 106 p. $1.00. 56.7 Su1B
TAYLOR, D. W. Fundamentals of soil mechanics. New
York, Wiley, 1948. 700 p. $6.00. 56.43 T21
THOMPSON, L. M. Soils and soil fertility. Dubuque,
Brown, 1950. 254 p. $5.00. 56 T37
TRUOG, E., ed. Mineral nutrition of plants. Madison,
Wis. Press, 1951. 469 p. $6.00. 463.34 T77
VAN SLYKE, L. L. Fertilizers and crop production. New
York, Orange Judd, 1932. 493 p. $4.00. 57 V36F
WEIR, W. W. Soil science, its principles and practice.
Rev. ed. Philadelphia, Lippincott, 1949. 615 p.
$5.00. 56 W43
WORTHEN, E. L. Farm soils; their management and
fertilization. Ed. 4. New York, Wiley, 1948. 510 p.
$3.60. 56.7 W89

CONSERVATION OF NATURAL RESOURCES

BENNETT, H. H. Elements of soil conservation. New
York, McGraw-Hill, 1947. 406 p. $3.20. 56.7 B43E
BENNETT, H. H. Soil conservation. New York, McGraw-
Hill, 1939. 993 p. $6.50. 56.7 B43S
BRINK, W. Big Hugh, the father of soil conservation.
New York, Macmillan, 1951. 167 p. $2.75. 120 B43
CARHART, A. H. Water-or your life. Philadelphia,
Lippincott, 1951. 312 p. $3.50. 292 C192
CHAPMAN, P. W., FITCH, F. W. Jr., and VEATCH, C. L.,
eds. Conserving soil resources; a guide to better
living. Atlanta, Smith, 1950. $3.28. 56.7 C36
CHASE, S. Rich land, poor land; a study of waste in the
natural resources of America. New York, McGraw-
Hill, 1936. 261 p. $5.00. 279 C34
ELLIOTT, C. N. Conservation of American resources.
Atlanta, Smith, 1951. 430 p. $3.39. 279.12 E15
FRANK, B., and NETBOY, A. Water, land, and people.
New York, Knopf, 1950. 331 p. $4.00. 292 F85
GRAHAM, E. H. Natural principles of land use. New
York, Oxford U. Press, 1944. 274 p. $4.50. 282 G76
GUSTAFSON, A. F., and others. Conservation in the
United States. Ed. 3. Ithaca, Comstock, 1949. 534 p.
$5.00. 279.12 G97
C. H. Guise, W. J. Hamilton Jr., and H. Ries, joint
authors.
MEZERIK, A. G. The pursuit of plenty; the story of
man's expanding domain. New York, Harper, 1950.
209 p. $3.00. 280.12 M57P
OSBORN, F. Our plundered planet. Boston, Little,
Brown, 1948. 217 p. $2.50. 279 Os1
PEARSON, F. A., and HARPER, F. A. The world's hun-
ger. Ithaca, Cornell U. Press, 1945. 90 p. $1.50.
389 P313W
SEARS, P. B. Deserts on the march. Ed. 2. Norman, U.
Okla. Press, 1947. 178 p. $2.75. 277.12 Se1
SHEPARD, W. Food or famine; the challenge of erosion.
New York, Macmillan, 1945. 225 p. $4.00.
56.7 Sh4F
SMITH, G. H., ed. Conservation of natural resources.
New York, Wiley, 1950. 552 p. $6.00. 279.12 SmS
VAN DERSAL, W. R. The American land; its history and
its uses. New York, Oxford U. Press, 1943. 215 p.
$4.00. 282.12 V28
VAN DERSAL, W. R., and GRAHAM, E. H. The land re-
newed; the story of soil conservation. New York,
Oxford U. Press, 1946. 109 p. $2.00. 56.7 V28
VOGT, W. Road to survival. New York, Sloane, 1948.
335 p. $4.00. 279 V86
WHITAKER, J. R., and ACKERMAN, E. A. American
resources, their management and conservation. New
York, Harcourt, Brace, 1951. 497 p. $6.75; text ed.
$4.50. 279.12 W58

IRRIGATION AND DRAINAGE

AYRES, Q. C., and SCOATES, D. Land drainage and reclamation. Ed. 2. New York, McGraw-Hill, 1939.
496 p. $5.00. 54 Ay7
ETCHEVERRY, B. A. Irrigation practice and engineering. V. 1, Use of irrigation water and irrigation
practice, by B. A. Etcheverry and S. T. Harding. Ed.
2, 1933. V. 2, Conveyance of water. 1915. V. 3, Irrigation structures and distribution, 1916. New York,
McGraw-Hill, 1915-1933.
V. 1, $5.00; v. 2, $6.00, v. 3, $6.50.
HOUK, I. E. Irrigation engineering. V. 1, Agricultural

and hydrological phases. New York, Wiley, 1951.
545 p. $9.00. 290 H81
ISRAELSEN, O. W. Irrigation principles and practices.
Ed. 2. New York, Wiley, 1950. 405 p. $6.00.
55 Is7
PICKELS, G. W. Drainage and flood-control engineering.
Ed. 2. New York, McGraw-Hill, 1941. 476 p. $4.50.
54 P58
ROE, H. B. Moisture requirements in agriculture; farm
irrigation. New York, McGraw-Hill, 1950. 413 p.
$5.50. 55 R62
THORNE, D. W., and PETERSON, H. B. Irrigated soils:
their fertility and management. Philadelphia,
Blakiston, 1949. 288 p. $5.00. 56.7 T393
WOOLEY, J. C., and BEASLEY, R. P. Farm water man-
agement. Columbia, Mo., Lucas Bros., 1950. 170 p.
$3.25. 292 W88

FARM BUILDINGS AND
AGRICULTURAL MACHINERY

BARRE, H. J., and SAMMET, L. L. Farm structures.
New York, Wiley, 1950. 650 p. $7.50. 296 B27
CARTER, D. G., and FOSTER, W. A. Farm buildings.
Ed. 3. New York, Wiley, 1941. 404 p. $4.00.
296 F81
COOK, G. C., SCRANTON, L. L., and McCOLLY, H. F.
Farm mechanics, text and handbook. Rev. Ed.
Danville, Interstate, 1951. 708 p. $4.50. 58 C772
THE HOME mechanic's handbook; and encyclopedia of
tools, materials, methods, and directions. New York,
Van Nostrand, 1945. 804 p. $6.95. 323 H75
JOHNSON, E. J., and HOLLENBERG, A. H. Servicing and
maintaining farm tractors. New York, McGraw-Hill,
1950. 313 p. $3.75. 58 J63
JONES, F. R. Farm gas engines and tractors. Ed. 2.
New York, McGraw-Hill, 1938. 486 p. $4.75.
58 J71
JONES, M. M. Shopwork on the farm. New York,
McGraw-Hill, 1945. 486 p. $3.50. 58 J72S
MORRISON, I. G. Farm tractor maintenance. Danville,
Interstate, 1946. 202 p. $2.80. 58 M83F
MORRISON, I. G. Repairing farm machinery. Danville,
Interstate, 1940. 181 p. $2.80. 58 M83
POPULAR MECHANICS MAGAZINE. Farm manual.
Chicago, Popular Mechanics Press, 1948. 284 p.
$3.00. 389.25 P81
PUTNAM, P. C. Power from the wind. New York, Van
Nostrand, 1948. 224 p. $6.00. 335 P98
ROEHL, L. M. The farmer's shop book. Ed. 9.
Milwaukee, Bruce, 1950. 473 p. $3.25. 58 R62F
ROEHL, L. M. Fitting farm tools. Ed. 3. Milwaukee,
Bruce, 1940. 120 p. $1.00. 58 R62Fi
SMITH, H. P. Farm machinery and equipment. Ed. 3.
New York, McGraw-Hill, 1948. 520 p. $5.00.
58 Sm5
STONE, A. A. Farm machinery. Ed. 3. New York,
Wiley, 1942. 524 p. $3.75. 58 St7
SUCCESSFUL FARMING. Building book. Des Moines,
The author, 1947. 70 p. $.50. 296 Su1B
TURNER, A. W., and JOHNSON, E. J. Machines for the
farm, ranch and plantation. New York, McGraw-Hill,
1948. 793 p. $6.00. 58 T85
WOOLEY, J. C. Farm buildings. Ed. 2. New York,
McGraw-Hill, 1946. 354 p. $4.00. 296 W88
WRIGHT, F. B. Rural water supply and sanitation. Ed.
3. New York, Wiley, 1950. 380 p. $3.24. 335 W932

RURAL ELECTRIFICATION

EARP, U. F. Rural electrification engineering. New
York, McGraw-Hill, 1950. 313 p. $3.50. 335 Ea7
EDISON ELECTRIC INSTITUTE. FARM SECT. Farm
electrification manual. New York, The author,
1946-51. 17 sections, loose-leaf, with binder. $9.45
335 Ed422
RICHTER, H. P. Practical electrical wiring. Ed. 3.
New York, McGraw-Hill, 1947. 574 p. $3.75.
335 R41Pe
SCHAENZER, J. P. Rural electrification. Ed. 4. Mil-
waukee, Bruce, 1948. 338 p. $3.75. 335 Sch1
WRIGHT, F. B. Electricity in the home and on the farm.
Ed. 3. New York, Wiley, 1950. 380 p. $3.96.
335 W932

AGRICULTURAL ECONOMICS

APP, F., and WALLER, A. G. Farm economics, management and distribution. Ed. 3. Philadelphia, Lippincott, 1938. 700 p. $5.50. 281 Ap4

BLACK, J. D., and KIEFER, M. E. Future food and agriculture policy; a program for the next ten years. New York, McGraw-Hill, 1948. $4.25. 281 B56F

BLACK, J. D. Rural economy of New England; a regional study; with the assistance of the Committee on research in the Social Sciences and the Graduate School of Public Administration of Harvard University. Cambridge, Harvard U. Press, 1950. 796 p. $7.50, text ed. $5.75. 281.004 B56

BRANDT, K. The reconstruction of world agriculture. New York, Norton, 1945. 416 p. $4.00. 281 B733

DUMMEIER, E. F., HEFLEBOWER, R. B., and NORMAN, T. Economics with applications to agriculture. Ed. 3. New York, McGraw-Hill, 1950. 718 p. $5.00. 281 D89

EZEKIEL, M., ed. Towards world prosperity, through industrial and agricultural development and expansion. New York, Harper, 1947. 455 p. $5.50. 280 Ez3

FORSTER, G. W., and LEAGER, M. C. Elements of agricultural economics. New York, Prentice-Hall, 1950. 441 p. $6.65. 281 F772E

FULMER, J. L. Agricultural progress in the Cotton Belt since 1920. Chapel Hill, U. N. C. Press, 1950. 236 p. $3.50. 281.002 F95

GOLD, B. Wartime economic planning in agriculture; a study in the allocation of resources. New York, Columbia U. Press, 1949. 595 p. $6.75. 281.12 G56

HIBBARD, B. H. Agricultural economics. New York, McGraw-Hill, 1948. 441 p. $5.00. 281.12 H52

JESNESS, O. B., ed. Readings on agricultural policy, assembled and published under the sponsorship of the American Farm Economic Association. Philadelphia, Blakiston, 1949. 470 p. $4.75. 281.12 J49R

JOHNSON, D. G. Trade and agriculture; a study of inconsistent policies. New York, Wiley, 1950. 198 p. $2.50. 286 J632

MIGHELL, R. L., and BLACK, J. D. Interregional competition in agriculture; with special reference to dairy farming in the Lake States and New England. Cambridge, Mass., Harvard U. Press, 1951. 320 p. $5.00. 281.12 M58

ROSS, R. C. Introduction to agricultural economics. New York, McGraw-Hill, 1951. 414 p. $5.00. 281.12 R73

SCHULTZ, T. W. Agriculture in an unstable economy. New York, McGraw-Hill, 1945. 229 p. $3.00. 281.12 Sch82A

TAYLOR, H. C. Outlines of agricultural economics. Rev. ed. New York, Macmillan, 1931. 614 p. $4.50. 281 T210

WILCOX, W. W., and COCHRANE, W. W. Economics of American agriculture. New York, Prentice-Hall, 1951. 594 p. $7.35. 281.12 W64E

Agricultural Credit

DUGGAN, I. W., and BATTLES, R. U. Financing the farm business. New York, Wiley, 1950. 354 p. $4.00. 284.2 D872

MURRAY, W. G. Agricultural finance. Ed. 2. Ames, Iowa State Col. Press, 1947. 328 p. $4.00. 284.2 M96

MURRAY, W. G. Farm appraisal; classification and valuation of farm land and buildings. Ed. 2. Ames, Iowa State Col. Press, 1947. 278 p. $3.00. 282 M96

NORTON, L. J. Financing agriculture. Rev. ed. Danville, Interstate, 1948. 434 p. $4.00. 284.2 N82

Agricultural Prices

JOHNSON, D. G. Forward prices for agriculture. Chicago, U. Chicago Press, 1947. 259 p. $3.00. 284.3 J63

SHEPHERD, G. S. Agricultural price analysis. Ed. 3. Ames, Iowa State Col. Press, 1950. 279 p. $3.50. 284.3 Sh4Ag

SHEPHERD, G. S. Agricultural price policy. Ed. 2. Ames, Iowa State Col. Press, 1947. 440 p. $4.50. 284.3 Sh4A

THOMSEN, F. L. Agricultural prices. New York, McGraw-Hill, 1936. 471 p. $4.50. 284.3 T38

WAITE, W. C., and TRELOGAN, H. C. Agricultural market prices. Ed. 2. New York, Wiley, 1951. 440 p. $5.25. 284.3 W13

Cooperatives

BAKKEN, H. H., and SCHAARS, M. A. The economics of cooperative marketing. New York, McGraw-Hill, 1937. 583 p. $5.50. 280.2 B172

BLANKERTZ, D. F. Marketing cooperatives. New York, Ronald, 1940. 488 p. $4.50. 280.2 B61

INFIELD, H. F. Cooperative communities at work. New York, Dryden Press, 1945. 201 p. $3.00. 282.2 In32

NOURSE, E. G., and KNAPP, J. G. The cooperative marketing of livestock. Washington, Brookings, 1931. 486 p. $3.50. 280.3 N86C

PACKEL, I. Law of the organization and operation of cooperatives. Ed. 2. Albany, Bender, 1947. 389 p. $7.50. 280.2 P12

TURNER, P. They did it in Indiana; the story of the Indiana Farm Bureau co-operatives. New York, Dryden, 1947. 159 p. $2.25. 280.2 T854

WIETING, C. M. The progress of cooperatives, with aids for teachers. New York, Harper, 1952. 210 p. $3.00. 280.2 W63P

Farm Management

BLACK, J. D., and others. Farm management. New York, Macmillan, 1947. 1073 p. $5.75. 281.12 B56F M. Clawson, C. R. Sayre, and W. W. Wilcox, joint authors.

EFFERSON, J. N. Farm records and accounts. New York, Wiley, 1949. 281 p. $3.25. 30.6 Ef3

FORSTER, G. W. Farm organization and management. Rev. ed. New York, Prentice-Hall, 1946. 409 p. $5.35; text ed. $4.50. 281.12 F77

HALL, I. F., and MORTENSON, W. P. The farm management handbook. Danville, Interstate, 1948. 576 p. $3.15. 281.12 H14

HART, V. B., and WARREN, S. W. Farm management manual. Ed. 2. Ithaca, Comstock, 1951. 86 p. $2.00. 281.12 H25

HART, V. B., BOND, M. C., and CUNNINGHAM, L. C. Farm management and marketing. New York, Wiley, 1942. 637 p. $3.24. 281 H25

HOPKINS, J. A. Elements of farm management. Ed. 3. New York, Prentice-Hall, 1947. 524 p. $5.65. 281 H77E

HOPKINS, J. A., and HEADY, E. O. Farm records. Ed. 3. Ames, Iowa State Col. Press, 1949. 303 p. $3.75. 30.6 H77F

JOHNSON, S. E., and others. Managing a farm. New York, Van Nostrand, 1946. 365 p. $3.75; text ed. $3.00. 281.12 J62 N. W. Johnson, O. J. Scoville, M. R. Cooper, and S. W. Mendum, joint authors.

ROBERTSON, L. S., and WOODS, R. H. Farm business management. Revised, Philadelphia, Lippincott, 1951. 546 p. $3.40. 281.12 R54

VAUGHAN, L. M., and HARDIN, L. S. Farm work simplification. New York, Wiley, 1949. 145 p. $2.80. 283 V46

Land Economics

BUNCE, A. C. Economics of soil conservation. Ames, Iowa State Col. Press, 1942. 227 p. $3.00. 56.7 B88

CLAWSON, M. Uncle Sam's acres. New York, Dodd, Mead, 1951. 414 p. $5.00. 282.12 C57

ELY, R. T., and WEHRWEIN, G. S. Land economics. New York, Macmillan, 1940. 512 p. $5.50. 282 EL9L

RENNE, R. R. Land economics; principles, problems, and policies in utilizing land resources. New York, Harper, 1947. 736 p. $5.00. 282 R29

SAUNDERSON, M. H. Western land and water use. Norman, U. Okla. Press, 1950. 217 p. $3.75. 282.003 Sa8

TIMMONS, J. F., and MURRAY, W. G., eds. Land problems and policies. Ames, Iowa State Col. Press [1950] 298 p. $4.00. 282 T48

Marketing

AGNEW, H. E., and HOUGHTON, D. Marketing policies. Ed. 2. New York, McGraw-Hill, 1951. 590 p. $6.50. 280.3 Ag6

BARTLETT, R. W. The milk industry; a comprehensive survey of production, distribution, and economic importance. New York, Ronald, 1946. 282 p. $4.50. 281.344 B28

BENJAMIN, E. W., PIERCE, H. C., and TERMOHLEN, W. D. Marketing poultry products. Ed. 4. New York, Wiley, 1949. 389 p. $6.00. 280.347 B43M

CLARK, F. E., and WELD, L. D. H. Marketing agricultural products in the United States. New York, Macmillan, 1932. 672 p. $6.50. 280.3 C54M

DOWELL, A. A., and BJORKA, K. Livestock marketing. New York, McGraw-Hill, 1941. 534 p. 280.340 D75

LARSON, A. L. Agricultural marketing. New York, Prentice-Hall, 1951. 519 p. $7.00, text ed. $5.25. 280.3 L322

- 14 -

LORIE, J. H., and ROBERTS, H. V. Basic methods of marketing research. New York, McGraw-Hill, 1951. 453 p. $6.50.' 280.3 L89

NORTON, L. J., and SCRANTON, L. L. Marketing of farm products; principles and problems for students of vocational agriculture, [Ed. 2] Danville, Interstate, 1949. 458 p. $2.50.

SHEPHERD, G. S. Marketing farm products. Ed. 2. Ames, Iowa State Col. Press, 1947. 461 p. $4.25. 280.3 Sh4M

THOMSEN, F. L. Agricultural marketing. New York, McGraw-Hill, 1951. 483 p. $6.00. 280.3 T36

RURAL SOCIOLOGY

HAYES, W. J. The small community looks ahead. New York, Harcourt, Brace, 1947. 276 p. $3.00. 280.12 H322

HITCH, E. V. Rebuilding rural America; new designs for community life. New York, Harper, 1950. 273 p. $3.50. 281.2 H63

LANDIS, B. Y. Rural welfare services. New York, Columbia U. Press, 1949. 201 p. $3.00. 280.12 L23R

LOOMIS, C. P., and BEEGLE, J. A. Rural social systems; a textbook in rural sociology and anthropology New York, Prentice-Hall, 1950. 873 p. $6.75. 281.2 L87R

MORGAN, A. E. The small community; foundation of democratic life; what it is and how to achieve it. New York, Harper, 1942. 312 p. $3.50. 281.2 M82

MOTT, F. D., and ROEMER, M. I. Rural health and medical care. New York, McGraw-Hill, 1948. 608 p. $6.50. 448 M853

NELSON, L. L. Rural sociology. New York, Amer. Book Co., 1948. 567 p. $5.25. 281.2 N332

OGDEN, J., and OGDEN, J. Small communities in action; stories of citizen programs at work. New York, Harper, 1946. 244 p. $3.00. 281.2 Og22

SANDERS, I. T. Making good communities better; a handbook for civic-minded men and women; with selected guideposts by seventeen authorities. Lexington, U. Ky. Press, 1950. 179 p. $2.00. 280 Sa52

TAYLOR, C. C., and others. Rural life in the United States. New York, Knopf, 1949. 549 p. $5.00. 281.2 T21R

D. Ensminger, T. W. Longmire, and W. C. McKain, joint authors.

AGRICULTURAL HISTORY

DIES, E. J. Titans of the soil; great builders of agriculture. Chapel Hill, U. N. C. Press, 1949. 213 p. $3.50. 119 D563

FRYER, L. N. American farmer; his problems and his prospects. New York, Harper, 1947. 172 p. $3.00. 281.12 F94

GRAS, N. S. B. History of agriculture in Europe and America. Ed. 2. New York, Appleton-Century-Crofts, 1940. 496 p. $4.00. 30.9 G762

HEDRICK, U. P. History of horticulture in America to 1860. New York, Oxford U. Press, 1950. 551 p. $7.50. 90.51 H35

KLOSE, N. America's crop heritage; the role of foreign plant introduction by the Federal government. Ames, Iowa State Col. Press, 1950. 156 p. $3.50. 30.9 K69

SHANNON, F. A. The farmer's last frontier: agriculture, 1860-1897. New York, Rinehart, 1945. 434 p. $4.50. 30.9 Sh1

U. S. DEPT. OF AGRICULTURE. An historical survey of American agriculture. The farmer's changing world, a brief chronology of American agricultural history. Reprint from pages 103-326 and 1184-1196 of the 1940 Yearbook of agriculture. Washington, The author, 1941. (Yearbook Separate No. 1783). free.
    Contents: The farmer's changing world, by F. F. Elliott; Old ideals versus new ideas in farm life, by P. H. Johnstone; American agriculture - the first 300 years, by E. E. Edwards; Agriculture in the World War period, by A. B. Genung; The development of agricultural policy since the end of the World War, by C. C. Davis; Appendix - A brief chronology of American agricultural history, compiled by D. C. Goodwin.

WENTWORTH, E. N. America's sheep trails; history, personalities. Ames, Iowa State Col. Press, 1948. 667 p. $10.00. 45 W48A

WILCOX, W. W. The farmer in the second world war. Ames, Iowa State Col. Press, 1947. 410 p. $4.00. 281.12 W64

AGRICULTURAL EXTENSION

BRUNNER, E. S., SAUNDERS; I. T., and ENSMINGER, D. Farmers of the world; the development of agricultural extension. New York, Columbia U. Press, 1945. 208 p. $2.50. 275.2 B83

KELSEY, L. D., and HEARNE, C. C. Cooperative extension work. Ithaca, N. Y., Comstock, 1949. 424 p. $4.00. 275.2 K29

RECK, F. M. The 4-H story; a history of 4-H Club work. Chicago, Natl. Comt. Boys and Girls Club Work, 1951. 308 p. $3.00. 275.2 R242

RURAL HANDICRAFTS

EATON, A. H. Handicrafts of New England. New York, Harper, 1949. 374 p. $5.00. 317 Ea8

EATON, A. H. Handicrafts of the Southern Highlands; with an account of the rural handicraft movement in the United States and suggestions for the wider use of handicrafts in adult education and in recreation. New York, Russell Sage Found., 1937. 370 p. $3.50. 283 Ea8

HAINES, R. E., ed. The home crafts handbook. New York, Van Nostrand, 1948. 1008 p. $6.95.

PATTEN, M. The arts workshop of rural America; a study of the rural arts program of the agricultural extension service. New York, Columbia U. Press, 1937. 202 p. $1.50. 280.6 P27

Academic Press, Inc., 125 East 23rd St., New York 10, N. Y.
Allied Fur Industries, 2227 W. 182nd St., Gardena, Calif.
American Animal Hospital Association, 5335 Touhy Ave., Skokie, Ill.
American Bee Journal, Hamilton, Ill.
American Book Co., 55 - 5th Ave., New York 3, N. Y.
American Forestry Association, 919 17th St., N. W., Washington, D. C.
American Potash Institute, Inc., 1102 16th St., N. W., Washington, D. C.
American Poultry Association, Davenport, Iowa
American Poultry Hatchery Federation, 15 West 10th St., Kansas City 6, Mo.
American Public Health Association, 1790 Broadway, New York 19, N. Y.
American Rabbit & Cavy Breeders Association, Inc., 4323 Murray Ave., Pittsburgh 6, Pa.
American Remount Association, 805 Otis Bldg., 810 18th St., N. W., Washington 6, D. C.
American Saddle Horse Breeders Association, Inc., Louisville, Ky.
W. B. Andrews, State College, Miss.
Appleton-Century-Crofts, Inc., 29-35 West 32d St., New York 1, N. Y.
Association of Official Agricultural Chemists, Box 540, Benjamin Franklin Station, Washington, D. C.
Bailey Hortorium, Cornell University, Ithaca, N. Y.
A. S. Barnes & Co., 232 Madison Ave., New York 16, N. Y.
Floyd Barnhart, Caruthersville, Mo.
M. Barrows & Co., Inc., 114 East 32d St., New York 16, N. Y.
Beacon Milling Co., Inc., Cayuga, N. Y.
Matthew Bender & Co., Inc., 109 State St., Albany 1, N. Y.
Blakiston Co., 1012 Walnut St., Philadelphia 5, Pa.
Brookings Institution, 722 Jackson Place, N. W., Washington 6, D. C.
William C. Brown Co., 915 Main St., Dubuque, Iowa
Bruce Publishing Co., 400 N. Broadway, Milwaukee 1, Wis.
Burgess Publishing Co., 426-428 South 6th St., Minneapolis 15, Minn.
Cheesemaker Book Co., 4225 Wanetah Trail, Madison 5, Wis.
Chemical Publishing Co. Distributor is Haarlem Book Co.
Chronica Botanica, Box 151, Waltham 54, Mass.
Columbia University Press, 2960 Broadway, New York 27, N. Y.
Commonwealth Fund publications now published and distributed by Harvard University Press.
Comstock Publishing Co., Inc., 124 Roberts Pl., Ithaca, N. Y.
Cornell Co-operative Society, Barnes Hall, Cornell Heights, Ithaca, N. Y.
Cornell University Press, 124 Roberts Pl., Ithaca, N. Y.
Crown Publishers, 419 Fourth Ave., New York 16, N. Y.
Davison Chemical Corporation, Charles & Fayette St., Baltimore 3, Md.
The John Day Co., 210 Madison Ave., New York 16, N. Y.
De La Mare Garden Books, Distributed by Dodd, Mead & Co., 432 Fourth Ave., New York 16, N. Y.
Denlinger's, 117 Hamilton Ave., Silver Spring, Md.
Devin-Adair Co., 23 East 26th St., New York 10, N. Y.
Didier Publishers, 660 Madison Ave., New York 21, N. Y.
Dodd, Mead & Co., 432 Fourth Ave., New York 16, N. Y.
Doubleday & Co., Inc., Garden City, N. Y.
Dryden Press, Inc., 31 W. 54th St., New York 19, N. Y.
Duell, Sloan & Pierce, 270 Madison Ave., New York 16, N. Y.
Edison Electric Institute, 420 Lexington Ave., New York 17, N. Y.
Alexander Eger, Inc., 21 East Van Buren St., Chicago, Ill.
W. R. Ewing, Box 248, South Pasadena, Calif.
J. C. Fehr, 1302 Woodlawn Ave., Indianapolis, Ind.
Wilfred Funk, Inc., 227 East 44th St., New York 17, N. Y.
Fur, Fish, and Game, 174 E. Long St., Columbus 15, Ohio.
Dr. L. C. Gale, P.O. Box 451, Concordia, Kans.
Garden City Publishing Co., Inc., Garden City, N. Y.
Gilcrest Angora Center, Foxon Road, East Haven 12, Conn.
Ginn & Co., Statler Bldg., Boston 17, Mass.
Greenberg, Publisher, 201 East 57th St., New York 22, N. Y.
Grossett & Dunlap, Inc., 1107 Broadway, at 24th St., New York 10. N. Y.

W. F. Guard, 2274 Yorkshire Road, Columbus 10, Ohio.
Haarlem Book Co., 221 Fourth Ave., New York 3, N. Y.
Harcourt, Brace & Co., Inc., 383 Madison Ave., New York 17, N. Y.
Harper & Brothers, 49 East 33rd St., New York 16, N. Y.
R. C. Hartman, Box 950, Redlands, Calif.
Harvard University Press, Pub. Dept., 44 Francis Ave., Cambridge 38, Mass.
D. C. Heath & Co., 285 Columbus Ave., Boston 16, Mass.
Hildreth Press, Bristol, Conn.
Paul B. Hoeber, Inc., 49 E.33rd St., New York 16, N. Y.
Henry Holt & Co., Inc., 257 Fourth Ave., New York 10, N. Y.
Houghton Mifflin Co., 2 Park St., Boston 7, Mass.
O. F. Hunziker, 103 Seventh Ave., LaGrange, Ill.
Industrial Publications Inc., 254 W. 31st St., New York 1, N. Y.
International Baby Chick Association. Name changed in 1951 to American Poultry Hatchery Federation.
International Publishing Co., Duluth, Minn.
Interscience Publishers, Inc., 250 Fifth Ave., New York 1, N. Y.
The Interstate, 19-27 North Jackson St., Danville, Ill.
Iowa State College Press, Press Building, Ames, Iowa.
Island Press Cooperative, Inc., 470 West 24th St., New York 11, N. Y.
Journal Press, Dairy Goat Journal, Columbia, Mo.
Orange Judd Publishing Co., 15 East 26th St., New York 10, N. Y.
B. F. Kaupp, 405 South 8th St., Minneapolis, Minn.
Alfred A. Knopf, Inc., 501 Madison Ave., New York 22, N. Y.
Lea & Febiger, 600 Washington Square, Philadelphia 6, Pa.
J. R. Leahy and P. Barrow, distributor is Cornell Cooperative Society
J. B. Lippincott Co., 227-231 South 6th Street, Philadelphia 5, Pa.
Lithotype Process Co., 523 Folsom St., San Francisco, Calif.
Little, Brown & Co., 34 Beacon St., Boston 6, Mass.
Livestock Services, Inc., 10 Watson Place, Columbia, Mo.
Longmans, Green & Co., Inc., 55 Fifth Ave., New York 3, N. Y.
Long's College Book Co., 1836 N. High St., Columbus 1, Ohio.
Lucas Brothers, 909 Lowry Street, Columbia, Mo.
McGraw-Hill Book Co., Inc., 330 West 42nd St., New York 18, N. Y.
David McKay Co., 225 Park Ave., New York 17, N. Y.
Macmillan Co., 60 Fifth Ave., New York 11, N. Y.
MacNair-Dorland Co., Inc., 254 West 31st St., New York 1, N. Y.
Medill McBride Co., 200 E. 37th St., New York 16, N. Y.
Meredith Publishing Co., Des Moines 3, Iowa.
Milk Industry Foundation, 1001 15th St., N. W., Washington 5, D. C.
Morrison Publishing Co., 409 Highland Ave., Ithaca, N. Y.
William Morrow & Co., Inc., 425 Fourth Ave., New York 16, N. Y.
National Committee on Boys and Girls Club Work, 59 E. Van Buren St., Chicago 5, Ill.
National Fertilizer Association, 616 Continental Building, Washington, D. C.
National Research Council, 2101 Constitution Ave., Washington 25, D. C.
North American Veterinarian, Box 872, Evanston, Ill.
W. W. Norton & Co., Inc., 101 Fifth Ave., New York, N. Y.
OSC Cooperative Association, Oregon State College, Corvallis, Oreg.
Olsen Publishing Co., Fifth and Cherry Sts., Milwaukee 12, Wis.
Oxford University Press, 114 Fifth Ave., New York 11, N. Y.
C. H. Pease, Caanan, Connecticut.
Pedology Publications, New Brunswick, N. J.
Pilsbury Publishers Inc., 10 W.33rd St., New York 1, N. Y.
Pitman Publishing Corp., 2 West 45th St., New York 19, N. Y.
Mrs. S. J. Plimpton, 10 Bancroft Tower Road, Worcester, Mass.
Popular Mechanics Press, 200 East Ontario St., Chicago 11, Ill.
Prentice-Hall, Inc., 70 Fifth Ave., New York 11, N. Y.
Princeton University Press, Princeton, N. J.

Public Administration Service, 1313 East 60th St., Chicago 37, Ill.
Reinhold Publishing Corp., 330 West 42nd St., New York 18, N. Y.
Rinehart & Co., Inc., 232 Madison Ave., New York 16, N. Y.
Ronald Press Co., 15 East 26th St., New York 10, N. Y.
A. I. Root Co., Medina, Ohio.
Russell Sage Foundation, 505 Park Ave., New York 22, N. Y.
Rutgers University Press, New Brunswick, N. J.
W. B. Saunders Co, 218 West Washington Square, Philadelphia 5, Pa.
Charles Scribner's Sons, 597 Fifth Ave., New York 17, N. Y.
Sheridan House, Inc., 257 Fourth Ave., New York 10, N. Y.
Simon & Schuster, Inc., 1230 Sixth Ave., New York 20, N. Y.
William Sloane Associates, 119 W. 57th St., New York 19, N. Y.
J. Smith, Route 2, Ft. Myers, Fla.
Turner E. Smith & Co., 441 West Peachtree St., N. E., Atlanta 3, Ga.
C. H. Spurway, 436 Division St., East Lansing, Mich.
Stackpole Co., Cameron and Kelker Sts., Harrisburg, Pa.
Successful Farming, 1716 Locust St., Des Moines, Iowa.
Textile Book Publishers, Inc., 303 Fifth Ave., New York 16, N. Y.
C. C. Thomas, 301-327 E. Lawrence Ave., Springfield, Ill.
W. R. Thompson, State College, Miss.
Tudor Publishing Co., 221 Fourth Ave., New York 3, N. Y.
Udall Publishing Co., 106 Brandon Pl., Ithaca, N. Y.
United Duroc Record Association, 237-9 North Monroe St., Peoria 3, Ill.
U. S. Department of Agriculture, Washington 25, D. C.

U. S. Government Printing Office, Washington 25, D. C.
University of California Press, Berkeley 4, Calif.
University of Chicago Press, 5750 Ellis Avenue, Chicago 37, Ill.
University of Georgia Press, Athens, Ga.
University of Kentucky Press, McVey Hall, Lexington 29, Ky.
University of Minnesota Press, 10 Nicholson Hall, Minneapolis 14, Minn.
University of Nebraska Press, Lincoln, Nebr.
University of North Carolina Press, Chapel Hill, N. C.
University of Oklahoma Press, Norman, Okla.
University of Pennsylvania Press, 3436 Walnut St., Philadelphia 4, Pa.
University of Wisconsin Press, 811 State St., Madison 5, Wis.
D. Van Nostrand Co., Inc., 250 Fourth Ave., New York 3, N. Y.
Ives Washburn, Inc., 29 West 57th St., New York 19, N. Y.
Watt Publishing Co., Mount Morris, Ill.
Webb Publishing Co., 55 E. Tenth St., St. Paul 2, Minn.
West Virginia University Bookstore, Morgantown, W. Va.
Westernlore Press, 5040 Eagle Rock Blvd., Los Angeles 41, Calif.
G. R. White, 206 12th Ave., S. Nashville 2, Tenn.
John Wiley & Sons, Inc., 440 Fourth Ave., New York 16, N. Y.
Williams & Wilkins Co., Mount Royal and Guilford Aves., Baltimore 2, Md.
C. O. Williamson, New Plymouth, Idaho.
Windsor Press Division of Popular Mechanics Press, 200 East Ontario St., Chicago 11, Ill.
Yale University Press, 143 Elm St., New Haven 7, Conn.
Ziff-Davis Publishing Co., 185 North Wabash Ave., Chicago 1, Ill.

AUTHOR INDEX

Lightning Source UK Ltd.
Milton Keynes UK
UKHW011153051118
331792UK00005B/134/P

9 780260 458995